BUCKLEITNER'S
Guide to Using Tablets
with Young Children

Warren Buckleitner, PhD

D1472964

Gryphon House
www.gryphonhouse.com

Published by Gryphon House Inc.
P. O. Box 10, Lewisville, NC 27023
800.638.0928; 877.638.7576 (fax)
Visit us on the web at www.gryphonhouse.com.

Bulk Purchase
Gryphon House books are available for special premiums and sales promotions as well as for fund-raising use. Special editions or book excerpts also can be created to specifications. For details, call 800.638.0928.

Disclaimer
Gryphon House Inc. cannot be held responsible for damage, mishap, or injury incurred during the use of or because of activities in this book. Appropriate and reasonable caution and adult supervision of children involved in activities and corresponding to the age and capability of each child involved are recommended at all times. Do not leave children unattended at any time. Observe safety and caution at all times.

Library of Congress Cataloging-in-Publication Data
The Cataloging-in-Publication Data is registered with the Library of Congress for 978-0-87659-461-2.

DEDICATION

To my daughters, Sarah and Jenna. You have been my best teachers.

ACKNOWLEDGMENTS

This book would not have been possible without the patience and encouragement of my editors, Diane Ohanesian and Terrey Hatcher of Gryphon House, and the overworked staff at Children's Technology Review and the Mediatech Foundation.

CONTENTS

INTRODUCTION

Using tablets with preschool-age children holds great promise for learning and fun. But there's a price to pay. It seems to also inspire concern and questions among adults charged with a child's care and well-being. I wrote this guide to ease this stress with good information—namely, easy-to-read tips and objective reviews of the best apps you can get. Think of this book as your trusted trail guide as you navigate this new terrain with your children.

If you're already comfortable with technology, you may think that using technology with a child means visiting a toy store and buying one of the many $100 "kids' tablets." Not so fast!

Today's tablets are powerful devices, and quality varies. They can play many roles in a child's life, for better or for worse. The outcome depends on which tablet you choose, the apps (or software programs) you put on it, and the context you create for its use.

This single device generically called a tablet can also be a movie camera, video game, artist's easel, or a million-channel TV. It can be a savior for a struggling student by providing interactive tutorials that can break down a tricky math concept or a set of spelling problems into simple steps. Or it can be nothing more than a distraction that absorbs hours of valuable time each day that could be spent more productively.

By sharing my expertise based on more than 20 years of experience with children's interactive media, I aim to help you make those important decisions to encourage children's play and learning.

As the editor of Children's Technology Review (CTR), I continually evaluate interactive media for young children. Two other teachers and I started CTR in 1993 after witnessing the explosion of children's software. CTR has grown from a small newsletter for colleagues into a powerful online database. By serving as an independent authority on children's technology, CTR has helped many parents, teachers, and librarians make educated choices about apps, video games, toys, and websites.

In 2001, we created the Dust or Magic Institute, an annual meeting of designers, researchers, and reviewers, with the intention to share examples of best practices in children's digital media. Besides those ventures, I spent ten years covering children's technology for the *New York Times*. All that experience goes into the recommendations I make in this publication to help you choose technology wisely for the children in your care.

Before I begin, I would like to share a few important notes:

- This book is designed to be dynamic. New apps arrive every day. Therefore, in each section I link to a continually updated set of reviews in Children's Technology Review Exchange (CTREX). The links appear under icons labeled Stay Up to Date. They lead to a summary list. The links are designed to give you access to part of the list that contains the newer titles. To see the complete lists, you will need to be a paid subscriber to CTREX.

- I want my readers to know that I have no financial interest in any hardware or software company listed in this book. I've written this book from the point of view of a parent and teacher who puts the child first, always, ahead of the technology.

- You'll notice that many of the apps listed in this book run on Apple Products (primarily the iPad). I believe that hardware is only as good as the software it runs. As of this book's publishing date, the iPad is the best overall children's computing platform, by far. This may change in the future, and I've made every effort to describe the differences between various platforms to help you make the most out of what you might have.

Finally, successful use of technology must always start with an understanding of the child's age, interests, and individual abilities. So while you are using this publication to learn about technology, it is important to keep learning about the children in your care and make choices that reflect that knowledge.

Advice about Using Tablets

Putting a tablet in front of a child isn't enough. It's how you use this tool that matters. Here is a case in point from my experience with my seatmates during a trans-Atlantic flight.

I slid into the middle section of a Boeing 787, mentally ready for a seven-hour trans-Atlantic flight home. As a frequent flyer, I've learned to strategically choose my seat to increase the probability of having an empty one next to me. I was eager to spread out some work, plug into the AC power outlet, and get some writing done.

At first glance, I thought my scheme had worked. The middle section looked vacant. But a second glance shattered my work plans. It was filled by Nathan, age two years and three months. He was shy, smiling, and quickly retreated into his mother's arms. He soon returned my smile and shortly thereafter was exploring my earlobe. This was followed by a jumping session on his seat cushion that he had turned into a trampoline.

His mother was horrified. As we pulled back from the gate, she explained, extremely apologetically, that they were on their way to see Nathan's grandparents in Latrobe, Pennsylvania, for some quality bonding time. Although Nathan was used to traveling in airplanes, his mother noted something that every passenger in our section of the plane understood, "Seven hours is a long time."

"Yes, it is," I said with an understanding wink as I silently groped for the power outlet. I was determined to get some writing done anyway. I plugged in and employed "operation ignore Nathan" as I organized my computer work.

Out of the corner of my eye, I could see Nathan's mother rummaging through her "keep Nathan busy" bag. She seemed well prepared, with no-fail snacks, various toys, Nathan's cherished stuffed bear, and his special blanket. But there was one more thing. As soon as we were in the air, she pulled out her white iPad Mini in a leather case—the kind not made for kids—and set it up on Nathan's tray. "Don't worry," she said to me. "I've downloaded five of his favorite movies." The Disney-Pixar movie *Toy Story 3* was just starting, and for a few minutes I thought she was right.

But he wasn't fine. He had obviously seen the movie before. Even Buzz and Woody couldn't hold the attention of this wriggly two-year-old. Nathan started to do what normal two-year-olds do . . . move. The iPad kept falling, first back and then on the floor, and at one point, it ended up one row behind us.

Nathan found a solution. He turned around, sat on his serving tray, and then propped the iPad on his seat. From this position, he soon started a game of peekaboo with the passengers in the row behind us, forgetting the movie completely. Then he started playing with all the buttons within his reach, turning the overhead light on and off and calling the flight attendant.

It became clear that I wasn't going to get much work done on this flight. Out of self-preservation and for the good of the others, I took out my iPad and showed him an app called My Very Hungry Caterpillar, by StoryToys. The caterpillar was waiting, hungry, and—like Nathan—growing bored. It followed my finger around the screen, so I started talking to it, as if I were talking to a pet. "So . . . how do you like flying on an airplane, little caterpillar?" I asked. "Are you still hungry?"

I started picking fruit from one of the trees, and Nathan's small hand reached over to my iPad, attracted by one of Eric Carle's beautiful green and yellow pears. We were just reaching our cruising altitude when a spark of magic happened.

My Very Hungry Caterpillar ©2015 StoryToys. Used with permission.

The instant Nathan's finger touched the screen, the pear popped off the tree and fell to the ground. "Apple!" he cried, with a huge smile. To Nathan, even the pears and the plums were apples, but the hungry caterpillar didn't care. It kept eating as Nathan and I took turns plucking fruit. No words, lessons, or tutorials were exchanged between Nathan and me. We just played.

I could tell that Nathan was in the very early stages of learning to interact with a touch screen. Up to this point in his short life, iPads had mostly displayed moving pictures for passive watching. The idea that he could interact with the characters on the screen seemed extremely exciting to him. He jabbed faster and squealed louder. His instinct was if he pressed harder, he would get the result more quickly, and he was not so good with swiping.

In five minutes, my iPad had moved from my seat to Nathan's, and he had mastered the swipe. My hungry caterpillar was now Nathan's very hungry, very curious, very busy caterpillar. My app kept Nathan's fingers busy and his mind engaged with new ideas. His mother obviously preferred this type of screen time to the passive Disney watching that was the only other alternative. And after three hours, Nathan was asleep with a happy smile. So was his mother. When we landed, Nathan's mom asked me for the name of the app that had transformed her child and our flight.

Choosing an Appropriate Tablet

Before buying apps, you have to carefully consider which tablets will work best for the children who will use them. You can choose among Android models from many different manufacturers, which run Google's Android operating system, and Apple's different iPad models, which run Apple's iOS operating system.

Screen Size

One factor is screen size; you generally have three options when choosing mobile devices for children:

- **Small (a 4- to 6-inch screen, measured diagonally)—** These devices include phones and the iPod Touch, which can easily fit in a child's hand and may feel more personal.

- **Medium (a 6- to 9-inch screen)—**This category includes the Kindle, iPad Mini, most Android Kids Tablet models (Nabi, Kurio), and Samsung Galaxy Tab Kids Edition models.

- **Large (a 10- or 13-inch screen)—**Options include the regular iPad, the iPad Pro, and various Android models such as the Samsung Galaxy Tab.

Each size has unique characteristics, but for a younger child, regular-iPad-sized screens deliver the most bang for the buck. That's because most children's apps were designed with this screen size in mind. Screen fonts are the right size, and navigation icons are slightly larger.

Internal Storage

Another consideration is the amount of storage. Many non-iPad tablets, such as the Amazon Fire, come with a fixed amount of internal memory measured in gigabytes (GB). In 2015, the average size of a child's app was about 130 megabytes (MB), with a range of 30 MB to 987 MB. To put this in context, a really big app can take up as much as 1 GB of space. Most educational apps are much smaller, about 50 MB (meaning 20 could fit into 1 GB).

A movie like the HD version of *Toy Story* takes up about 5 GB of storage. With most iPads, you have the choice of 16, 32, 64, or 128 GB of memory, with a price range of $400 to $900. Most low-cost Android tablets come with only 8 GB of built-in memory, but they tend to offer some sort of expansion slot. If so, you can increase this built-in storage using an SD or a micro SD card. A 16 GB card costs about $10.

How much do you need? To find out, consider how many apps and videos you want to store on your device:

- Small, or 16 GB, can hold only three full-sized movies, 16 of the biggest apps, 123 average-size apps, or 800 of the smallest apps. But that doesn't leave much room for photos or music, which can easily eat up another 5 or 6 GB.

- Medium, or 32 GB, is the best balance between size and price, giving you the ability to store 246 average-sized apps.

- Large, or 64 GB, gives you 492 average-sized apps.

- Extra-large, or 128 GB, can hold about 984 average-sized apps.

Protective Case

Tablets are incredibly robust devices with no moving parts. My 2010 first-edition iPad has been dropped, stepped on, and attacked by dogs, and its battery has lived through hundreds of charges or partial charges, when plugged into different power sources all around the world. Sometimes it has hiccups, such as when I update the Apple operating system, iOS. But five years later as I write this, it is still being used in a classroom every day.

The biggest worry is dropping your tablet on a hard floor or having it transformed into a bathtub toy. There is no good solution to the bathtub situation except to make water play strictly off limits when using the tablet. However, you can protect against dropping by purchasing a silicone or rubber frame or a foam case made specifically for young children. Most Android tablets include a case in the purchase price.

When choosing protective covers, consider these questions:

- Does the case block important controls such as the on-off or volume buttons?

- Is the headphone jack easy to access?

- Is it hard to connect to the charging port?

- Does the case adequately protect the device?

- Can you easily snap the tablet in and out of the case?

In terms of protective cases for iPads, two brands stand out: Big Grips and Gripcase USA. Here is why:

- Gripcase by Gripcase-USA (www.gripcase-usa.com), ages three and up. On the plus side: Gripcase comes in five colors and has handles that can let you hang your iPad from a hook. The high-density foam generally doesn't block the key ports or speakers. Drawback: The case takes up a lot of room and makes the iPad harder to slip into a backpack. As with just about any case, you have to slip it off to find some of the ports.

- Big Grips Tweener and Big Grips Slim by KEM Ventures Inc. (www.biggrips.com), ages three and up. On the plus side: Big Grips Tweener is a thinner foam case designed for the iPad Mini; the Big Grips Slim is similar for the iPad. The case holds your iPad snuggly in a cushion of foam, greatly increasing the chance that it can survive even a dramatic fall. Of all the KEM foam cases, the Slim for the iPad and the Tweener for the iPad Mini offer the best combination of protection and portability.

Ideal Tablet Purchases

BUCKLEITNER RECOMMENDS

Get a regular-size iPad with two cameras and at the very least 32 GB of internal storage, if you can afford it. The front-facing camera is best for seeing your own face, and the rear-facing camera allows you to take photos and videos of other people and things while seeing what you are shooting. Despite costing more, this configuration will give you the biggest bang for your buck. An iPad Mini is the next best option. Reserve some money for a protective foam case and at least 50 apps, if you want to keep your purchase safe and keep it usable for the child.

If you prefer an Android, the Samsung Galaxy Tab Kids, for ages 3 and up, is hard to miss, with its bright orange and yellow case. It also stands at the head of the pack of current 7-inch tablets when it comes to some key factors—namely, ease of use, parental controls, and app selections—making it one of the better choices for children. This tablet offers access to just about everything Google—Google Mobile Services, Google Search, Gmail, Google Plus, YouTube, Google Talk, Google Maps, and especially the Google Play Store.

If you purchase a tablet with a capacitive touch screen, you will want to have a stylus as well. AppCrayon by Dano Toys is cheap (about $10), light, and fun to use. It works with any type of tablet or smartphone (Apple or Android) that has a capacitive touch screen. The triangle-shaped 4-inch stylus is made of soft rubber, with black strips of conductive material on the side that effectively transfer your hand's capacitive charge down to the black squishy stylus tip, essentially giving you an extension of your finger. The triangular shape is easy to grip and won't roll off the table. A loop on the end makes it possible to put it on a lanyard. The only drawback might be that children—and dogs—will want to chew on it. Just about any variety of stylus will be fine, however, and the most important judge is the child who will use it.

Replacing TV Time with App Time

Besides tablets and smartphones, you can consider another option: Apple TV 4th Generation ($150 and up). It offers a nice, hidden surprise for families: a growing number of apps that are compatible with Apple TV are showing up in the App Store. Seeing these app icons on your living room TV helps to blur the line between app time and video time. You can find video options from PBS Kids Video, StoryBots, and YouTube. But you can also find some interactive options. You can turn your screen into a giant planetarium with Star Walk Kids, or an interactive fairy tale with Sago Mini Fairy Tales. The offerings make it easier to turn that big screen into something to play with instead of just to watch. The

controllers, which you charge using your Apple-to-USB connector cable (just like an iPhone or iPad), connect to the TV using Bluetooth and are just as responsive as any game console. Besides the small Siri Remote that is included, you will probably want to buy the $50 Nimbus SteelSeries controller, which could easily be mistaken for a Microsoft Xbox or Sony PlayStation controller. This new generation of Apple TV also has built-in assistive technologies. Besides the ability to use voice search by having Siri in the remote, you can turn on a voice-over feature to have the menu icons read out loud.

Initial Use of Your Tablet

When using a new tablet for the first time, make sure you have a wireless network (wi-fi) connection. If any challenges arise, it usually helps to ask experienced users for advice and to search online for solutions to specific problems. As with any online research, make sure you're consulting reputable sources.

Touch-Screen Skills

Chances are that you can already use a touch screen effectively without classes or tutorials. Like the thousands of other skills a child acquires in the early years,

StoryBots Tap & Sing ©2015 JibJab Media. Used with permission.

touch screen skills come through playful exploration. Children begin handling tablets with jabs, and ultimately they become sufficiently skilled to use coordinated, multitouch gestures. The mastery of touch screens is a gradual process, as with speaking or writing. First, the child scribbles with crayons before learning to write with a pencil and paper. Gradually, with playful experimentation and formal learning, the child moves from scribbles to something resembling letters. Eventually, the child can produce words, sentences, and paragraphs. Similarly, touch screens require a combination of experimentation and some simple modeling from adults. Over time and with experience, children will learn how to interact in more sophisticated ways with touch screens.

As children spend time with responsive apps, they will become proficient, mastering more subtle techniques such as the swipe, the flick, the pinch and unpinch, and even the five-finger open and close. These two five-finger screen behaviors start with a fairly coordinated pincer grasp, a developmental skill that tends to appear at about twelve months of age. The reverse pincer grasp, called the "unpinch," appears much later. Children master both five-finger gestures only with plenty of experience, whether they are dealing with real objects, such as carrots or tidbits of cereal, or with responsive apps in the digital world.

Tablet Basics

When you first take a tablet out of the box and its design is unfamiliar, it can be difficult to do even simple tasks such as adjusting the volume or finding the plug to charge the battery. Before you try to turn on your new tablet, you might want to use an existing computer to view a how-to video on YouTube that explains your specific device and the basics for getting started. It helps to be familiar with the basics of turning on the hardware and opening software apps before you take the tablet out of the box.

For example, if you have an Android device, it may not have a physical home button, which allows you to exit from an app and return to the home screen. Android, an operating system currently developed by Google, powers a wide range of devices from different companies that tend to be much cheaper than Apple devices. However, fewer apps are available for Android devices, and some people find Android tablets harder to use than iPads. Because many Android devices do not have a physical home button, children can get trapped in an app. Some Android developers have compensated for these challenges by creating child-friendly shells that lay over the Android operating system. Shells can include features such as an app timer and the ability to create individual profiles for children.

One popular model is the Amazon Fire HD Kids Edition, which comes with an initial price that includes one year of access to thousands of books and videos. Although the app selection is again a fraction of the Apple offerings, the Fire's low price and higher-quality content library makes it worthy of consideration. Just remember that after the year is up, you will have to pay a monthly fee to continue your child's access. Also watch the amount of on-board storage. Some of the Amazon tablets have very little internal storage (just 8 GB) and no SD card expansion. This means that even though you might be able to buy lots of apps, music, books, and movies, you won't have the room to store a large amount. Amazon does offer a two-year, no-questions-asked guarantee for replacement if the child breaks the tablet.

Using the Apps

It is simple enough for children to open an app; they can tap the appropriate icon on the screen and start it up. But there are many more necessary navigation skills for fully capitalizing on tablets and apps. Like riding a bike or walking, children can't master these navigations skills just from being shown how to make the gestures with their fingers; they have to experiment and practice! So stock your tablet with responsive apps that instantly reward any touch with a meaningful response (see recommendations in Chapter 3).

Once you have a large assortment of apps, you and the child will need to know how to find a particular one. On an iPad, swipe down anywhere on the screen with one finger. A search option should appear with a keyboard. Of course, if the child does not yet know letters or can't type, you will need to help with the search. Type a few letters of the title to see a list and tap the name to open it. Note that you can also search by the name of the app publisher. On an Android tablet, you can either download and install an app for app searching or search for an app from within the Google Play store. Start Google Play, and touch the magnifying glass in the My Apps column.

To delete an app on an iPad, hold your finger on the icon for a few seconds until it starts to wriggle. Touch the X to delete it. Press the home button to stop the apps from wriggling. If you accidentally delete an app, you should still have a copy floating around in the cloud, just in case you want to download it later.

To delete an app from an Android tablet, go to the device's settings menu and then go to the apps or application manager menu. Find the app you would like to remove, and click on the uninstall option.

For a child's very first screen experience, choose an app like Sago Mini Music Box from Canadian publisher Sago Sago Toys, where any touch on the screen makes a sound. Of course, there's also My Very Hungry Caterpillar by StoryToys. If it worked with Nathan for seven hours on an airplane, it might work for your child too.

STAY UP TO DATE

Use this link to check out CTREX reviews of other starter apps that are responsive and can help a child make the connection between their hand motions and activities on a screen.

http://bitly.com/1GpNI8N

Care and Safety

Think about setting aside a place for the children to use the tablet as you would other learning and play materials, such as a picture book or a tub of blocks. Put the tablet within their reach, and make sure it is near some sort of power outlet. You may find a spot for it on a table, in a clear container, or mounted on a wall. Make sure the children always know where to find and keep it.

Note that although there is little risk of a shock from the USB cables that connect the tablet to a power outlet, young children should not be plugging or unplugging electronic devices. Take the precaution of using safety plugs in all unused AC power outlets.

Sago Mini Music Box. ©2015 Sago Sago Toys. Used with permission.

If an app makes a sound when children touch the screen, they are more likely to keep experimenting and learning how to use the device.

After you put the tablet in its foam case, you can personalize it. You might want to put a family photo on the lock screen, which is the first screen you see. For the home screen—which is the background for all the app icons—don't use an image that is cluttered because it will be distracting to the eyes. You might want to stick with one of the built-in images. Make sure you have a high contrast between the app icons and the background.

Skip using a clear plastic screen cover. All tablets have a slippery surface that is intended to be self-cleaning. The surface is also designed to be childproof and scratch resistant. This hard screen has huge benefits for use with young children, whose fingers are commonly covered with some sort of slimy substance. The best way to clean the screen is with a soft cloth—I use my shirt sleeve. For the hard jobs, you can also use an extremely small squirt (just a few drops) of water with the cloth, taking care not to let moisture near any openings on the device.

Introducing a New App

The first time a child uses an app, a little guidance can go a long way. The best way to introduce a new concept is with something real—the more tangible, the better. As an all-knowing adult, it's incredibly tempting to take over and make sure it's done right. But that approach runs contrary to the way young children

learn. Remember Jean Piaget's well-known comment, the gist of which was: when you teach a child something, you take away forever his chance of discovering it for himself. Piaget's advice holds true for children's apps.

So how do you overcome the temptation? Use a tried-and-true teaching technique called guided discovery. As you point to an icon on the screen, ask the child, "What does that do?" That way, you point at the solution, but you don't tell the answer. You literally guide the child toward the discovery. Of course, it can be hard to watch a child struggle, but that can be when the learning is most significant. Strive for self-control instead of stepping in and taking over. Give children a bit of slack in the leash of learning. The paths they take might be different, but they also might be more interesting.

Before introducing the app to the child, try using it yourself. Become familiar with how the menus work, take note of any difficult spots, figure out how to control sound and files, and so on—all before you introduce it to the child.

In some cases, you can try modeling the app, using some self-talk. As you play with the app, think out loud so the child can see what you're doing. "I'm going to touch that bear . . . I wonder what will happen." Keep your tone informational rather than artificially enthusiastic; you're describing, not selling. When the time is right, let the child have a turn or take over what you're doing. While the child is playing, label what you see going on. If appropriate, play along and take turns.

Goldilocks and Little Bear ©2015 Nosy Crow Ltd. Used with permission.

Interactive stories allow children to make choices for how the tale plays out.

Remember, it works best to use guided discovery or simply put your hands in your pockets to allow the child the freedom to explore. If you would like, you can see an example on YouTube as I watch two-year-old Max play with the program Busy Shapes (https://www.youtube.com/watch?v=JDTmbHYvVYk&feature=youtube).

Handy Tips

Questions and problems are going to arise when you're using technology. When something goes wrong with your tablet, your go-to solution is to find a different computer or smartphone and type your specific problem into a search engine. You'll be surprised at how much help you can find. In this section, I also will share some advice for specific problems.

Childproofing Your Tablet

Before the child starts using the tablet, you will want to take steps to protect the investment. You will need to turn on password protection for your device and for the app store where you purchase and download. Through parental controls, you can set restrictions on which content ratings you allow for apps. This does not prevent children from seeing mature content when they search. However, you can restrict what they are able to buy or download. You can also remove the Internet browser if you would like.

The Google Play site provides information about setting parental controls on your devices that use the Google site. (Go to https://support.google.com/ and search for "parental controls.") Go to the Apple support site to read information on setting parental controls on iPads or iPhones and to find out how to turn off in-app purchases (https://support.apple.com/en-us/HT201304). Amazon Fire Kids Edition has some default settings to keep the content child-friendly, and Amazon provides information on setting parental controls on other Fire tablets (http://www.amazon.com/gp/help/customer/display.html?nodeId=201729930). Also consider your privacy settings and whether you want to turn off location services for some or all apps. Just be aware that some map and weather-related apps depend on these features.

Speedy Charging

Imagine this scenario: You're headed out the door for a car trip, and you reach under the sofa to find your child's tablet. But it's dead!

If this should happen to you, there are several ways you can speed the charging:

- **Use a large-sized charger.** Phone or tablet chargers generally come in two sizes, a smaller 5-watt size and a larger 15-watt size. The larger size has three times the power and the ability to charge the device faster. However, the larger size will speed up the charging process only on devices designed to draw more power from the higher-watt chargers. Not all phones will charge faster, but generally a tablet will.

- **Use airplane mode.** Go to the settings, and turn on airplane mode. This turns off the radio transmitter in the tablet, saving energy so your battery can charge faster.

- **Turn off apps.** Your tablet will charge faster if it's not busy doing other things.

- **Keep an external battery handy.** Options vary in price from about $15 to $40, and they range greatly in size. Most start at 10,000 milli-amps, which is enough to give you at least a few hours of power in a pinch.

Screen Cleaning

Many people think that when they touch a tablet screen, they're touching glass. But they are actually touching a thin, clear polymer that is coating a special type of hardened glass, which makes it oleophobic, or resistant to oils. Besides being strong and hard, the screen's surface is slippery compared to glass, so body oils would rather stick to your finger, where they belong, rather than the screen surface.

To check it out, put a drop of vegetable oil on the screen and smear it around a bit. You'll see that it forms tiny beads, like the water on a duck's back. So you can simply wipe it off with a dish towel. But you still may see smudges left over from gooey fingers.

Follow the manufacturer's instructions for screen cleaning, but generally, you should avoid harsh substances such as household cleaners, alcohol, acetone, ammonia, or any abrasive cleaner. Instead, turn off the tablet so you can see smudges easier, and use a microfiber cloth to wipe the screen. If you still have a smudge, you can add some moisture with a puff of breath and rub a bit longer without the pressure. You can also try a slight misting of distilled water with the cloth; just don't get any liquid near the edges or near any openings.

Dealing with Water Damage

Unfortunately, sometimes a child's tablet will get wet. This isn't likely to end well, because water and electronics don't mix. If this happens:

1. Dry off the device with an absorbent towel or cloth. Get as much water as possible out of the device. It can be risky to blow-dry or vacuum the tablet, as this moves the moisture around.

2. Place the device into a large bowl of dry rice for a day; it will draw the moisture out.

3. If the device still won't turn on, consider trying to change the battery. This process isn't for the faint of heart, however, because some tablet parts are glued together. You may want to take it to an authorized dealer.

If you do end up having to replace the hardware, you should still have a copy of all your content in the cloud, providing you've synced your tablet to a computer or downloaded the apps from the Amazon Appstore, Google Play, iTunes, or another app cloud storage service. In that case, your apps should be safe and sound, living on a server for the app store. As long as you have your screen name and password, you have a key to your virtual app storage closet.

Questions and Tips

This section covers some common challenges that arise when children are using tablets and suggests problem-solving strategies.

Limiting Time on an App

On an Android device, you can download a timer app for controlling the amount of time a child spends on an app. A feature called Guided Access in Settings on the iPad will allow this kind of control also. To find it, go to Settings, General, Accessibility, and then scroll to the Learning section. Tap Guided Access to turn it on. Basically, you will use a count-down timer that shuts the app off after the time limit that you set.

Avoiding an Accidental Exit from an App

You also might find it useful to limit how a child can exit an app.

On an iPad, if the child accidentally swipes the screen with four or five fingers, the entire app will move off the screen and get replaced with another app screen. This happens when a feature called Multitasking Gestures is turned on. This can result in tears, especially for a young child.

To see if your iPad has this setting turned on, touch the screen with all five fingers at once and swipe to the side. Does the entire screen slide with your motion? If so, your iPad has Multitasking Gestures turned on. To turn it off, go to Settings, General, and look for the multitasking option. Toggle it off. If your iPad is frequently used by younger children, it's probably smart to keep this option disabled.

Trouble-Shooting Problems

Let's face it—children are hard on gadgets. My two daughters and two dogs have managed to damage many things over the years, including many mobile phones and laptop-charging cables, and on one sad day, a laptop screen was shattered.

Here are some common issues that might arise with tablets:

- **Problem: The screen is cracked.** Under extreme cases, the screen will crack but still function. Remember that a screen is not really glass—it's a laminated, thin layer of extremely hard plastic and glass. So there's no danger of sharp edges. But sorry—a broken screen should be fixed professionally. The good news is that many independent screen-fixing shops are springing up and repair costs are dropping to around $100.

- **Problem: The tablet is frozen.** Hold the sleep-wake (or on-off) button for five seconds or so. For iPads, you should ideally see "slide to power off" appear. Use the button to restart your iPad, and it should be usable. For iPads or Android devices, doing a complete restart can help to clear out any glitches or frozen apps.

  If you can't turn off your device, you can try to reset it as a last resort. That involves pressing the sleep-wake button and home button for at least 10 seconds until the Apple logo appears on the screen.

- **Problem: The screen is dark, and the tablet won't respond to the on-off button.** To make sure the battery has some charge, plug it into the wall for at least fifteen minutes. If the tablet still won't turn on, use another device to find directions for resetting the tablet.

age-appropriate instructions and tasks that are at the right level. Here are some

Considerations When Choosing Apps

When choosing which programs you want children to use, you will juggle many competing factors. As you evaluate an app, you will want to consider whether it is easy to use and at the same time provides continual challenges for the child using it. As you try out the program yourself, consider whether the app has a responsive interface that will put the child in control and make it easy for the child to exit the activity when desired. I like to remind adults to look for the "DAP in the app." DAP means *developmentally appropriate practice*, or in other words, age-appropriate instructions and tasks that are at the right level. Here are some other factors to look for:

- Can you tailor the app to a specific child?

- Are there multiple levels that provide increasing challenges?

- Is the cost affordable?

- Can you adjust the volume or background music?

- If you take pictures or make drawings, can you save your work?

- Can children play in pairs or teams?

An app is merely another tool for learning and play, so a knowledgeable adult should make the decision about whether it merits a child's time. Avoid downloading apps that have the following pitfalls:

- Activities that are too hard or too easy

- Any type of design that traps a child in the activity

- Activities or messages that are loaded with gender or ethnic bias

- Heavy commercial agendas, licensed characters, and links to toys or movies

- Poor-quality graphics or music

- Narration that is hard to understand

- Offered for free with in-app purchases

Choosing Apps to Support Learning Styles

If all the people who had meaningful roles in a child's life got together for tea or coffee, you would need several chairs—for the parent, of course, and for the child's pediatrician, teacher, librarian, coach, music teacher, religion teacher, and school administrator, among other possibilities. Each person would have a different idea about the potential uses and misuses of these devices. The librarian might share a list of favorite e-books, and the pediatrician might offer words of caution about excessive screen time.

Teachers and parents likely would consider various child development theories.

Piaget's Stages

Understanding the stages of cognitive development that children go through is an important consideration. Jean Piaget, a researcher in biology and psychology, observed that children move through four stages as they explore and make sense of their world:

- **Sensorimotor stage**—From birth to about age two, children are egocentric, meaning they think everyone has the same perspective that they have. They gain recognition that they can take action to make something move, and they develop an understanding that objects exist independent of their actions.

- **Preoperational stage**—From about two to seven years old, children tend to focus on only one dimension of a problem or task and continue to be egocentric in the beginning of this stage. During this time, they learn to use language and other symbols to represent objects.

- **Concrete operational stage**—From about seven to eleven years old, children are able to use logic in dealing with physical objects; they can make deductions about general principles based on specific instances they encounter. They also begin to understand that breaking something down or rearranging pieces does not change its number, mass, volume, or length.

- **Formal operational stage**—From about age eleven and up, children begin to be able to think logically about abstract situations, do mathematical calculations, and think creatively.

Vygotsky's Zone of Proximal Development

Psychologist Lev Vygotsky believed that people learn through social interactions with others and then internalize the learning. His zone of proximal development (ZPD) is also an important consideration in choosing the best app for each child. He theorized that children learn best when they are given challenges along with guidance to help them gain the needed skills. If they can stretch themselves and achieve their goals with scaffolding from knowledgeable adults, then they are working within their ZPD.

Skinner's Reinforcement Theory

B. F. Skinner's reinforcement theory also is relevant to how an app might work to encourage learning. He observed that if a person's behavior is reinforced, then the person is more likely to repeat the action. That repetition then strengthens the behavior and encourages learning from the consequences of the action.

Technology as a Learning Tool

Given these different theory-driven views that can help determine the appropriate use or misuse of technology, keep in mind the following points:

- **Technology is powerful and has great potential for good or bad influences.** TVs, computers, cameras, phones, and timers of yesteryear have converged into one pocket-sized device. As I was reminded by Nathan on the plane, technology can be used to push content at a child to foster passivity (his mother's original plan), or it can be used to promote active play, problem solving, and busy fingers.

- **Every child is unique.** Children vary greatly by age, gender, and genetic makeup. My ability to match the best (or least worst) app with Nathan's level was influenced by my experience as an early childhood educator and my knowledge of apps. But he still might have rejected the caterpillar. Fostering happy, healthy children is an art; your chances of success will improve if you understand the technology and how children change as they grow.

- **Every learning and play setting is unique.** Schools and homes, and parenting and teaching styles are unique

cultural artifacts. No two are the same. This individuality makes it difficult to make app recommendations. The best app selections are made by adults who know the child.

• **We are the transitional parenting generation.** Thanks to the invention of the microprocessor, among other developments, the ways that children play and learn are very different from the playrooms and classrooms of the 1800s or 1900s. We have no choice but to accept this reality and do our best to figure it out, for the benefit of the next generation.

BUCKLEITNER RECOMMENDS

YouTube Kids

YouTube Kids is a free app for Android devices, iPads, and iPhones that is helping to redefine how children view TV and movies. YouTube Kids is owned by Google, which makes Android. But it runs on the iOS operating system as well.

If you are using YouTube Kids, you might find the following information helpful:

• YouTube Kids is free to download, but there is a catch. It serves up hundreds of advertisements and sponsored content in a soupy mix that includes full episodes of PBS programming. Videos can be posted by anybody, and content can include toys placed by a toy company. Even an adult can have trouble sorting out the sponsored content.

- YouTube Kids is like a free movie ticket to many children's shows. Try searching on "Mr. Rogers Neighborhood" or "The Lion King." You'll find full versions of just about every show within seconds. You'll like this app as much as your child does.

- You can turn off the annoying sound effects in the parents' menu, where you'll also find a timer that lets you limit the child's use to a certain number of minutes per day.

- There are two ways to search: typing or talking. The double-sized icons and voice search enhance both the finding and the browsing. Both are excellent language experiences.

- The results are filtered. The default filtering system takes a conservative view on obviously questionable words such as *boob* and *sex*, generating the message "try searching for something else!" The search word *reproduction* pulled up plenty of blush-free science-related videos on plant and cell division. I did find some pictures of nudes in a drawing tutorial and in images of historical sculptures, but the chances that a child will stumble upon something inappropriate are far smaller than when using the regular version of YouTube.

In reality, no search engine is perfect, so it is smart to keep an eye on every screen a child may be using, just as you would any magazine they might flip through or any news program that might be broadcasting. You may believe that watching six hours of kitten videos is unhealthy or that nude sketches by Renaissance artists are off limits. It's also possible to turn off searching in YouTube Kids, using features offered behind an age gate that requires reading numerals. But keep in mind that this is soft security; a motivated older child can hack through an age gate. Oftentimes, this is as easy as using a different device. So your job naturally is to set rules, use password protection when appropriate, and monitor children's use of technology.

Recommended Apps by Age and by Subject

Knowing which apps get good reviews from caregivers, teachers, and parents can be helpful as you consider which ones to buy or avoid for children's use. However, the online app stores continually update their offerings, so any information you have can quickly become out of date. It pays to get recommendations from multiple sources and then make your own educated decision. In this chapter, you will find app recommendations by age and by subject. To get more up-to-date information, you might choose to follow the links to the Children's Technology Review Exchange (CTREX) database, which is a collection of educational reviews of interactive media for children. Full access to CTREX requires a paid subscription; however, the links in this book offer readers limited access for free to supplement and refresh the information provided here.

As you give children new experiences with carefully selected apps and tablets, you are encouraging growth that will help them reach out in unforeseen directions. So, using a tree as a metaphor, it is like providing fertile ground to promote a healthy seedling. As the child experiments and learns, you never know where roots will grow or where their interests will take them. Amid uncertainty and a bit of guesswork, you do your best to clear a weed-free path toward success. That means choosing apps that are easy and fun to use and that offer continual opportunities for learning.

Over time, these apps will provide nutrients in the form of novel experiences that include time playing informally among friends and formal learning in school settings. New experiences will naturally give rise to new questions about why and how something works.

As children's learning branches out in unexpected directions, you can nurture that growth by exposing them to interesting experiences. One child might have a strong musical ability, another might enjoy physical games, and yet another might have mathematical aptitude. Or one child might have a bit of everything. Many parents want a child that is well rounded, with a variety

of skills and competencies. By providing challenging apps that tap a child's interests and help develop new skills, you promote opportunities for new branches, in the form of new skills, interests, and competencies.

As those interests and skills mature, children will be able to enjoy their accomplishments, which could be compared to the fruit on a tree.

As teachers, caregivers, and parents, we all want children to reach their full potential. With that goal in mind, let's look at some choices that could help them grow in multiple ways.

Apps by Age

A child's developmental level should be your first consideration when choosing any tool for play and learning. Just as you wouldn't buy a toddler a two-wheeler bike, you shouldn't download an app that could create a frustrating experience. As you consider which apps are best for particular children, think about how you would answer the following questions:

- What is the child's age?
- What are the child's interests and prior experiences?
- Will the apps be used at home, at school, or in a library?
- How much money do you want to spend?
- How much memory does the tablet have?
- Does the device have a camera?

If you would like to stock up on apps that will be age appropriate, check out some recommendations listed by age in the section that follows.

Ages Two and Younger

Now that tablets have touch screens and motion sensors, apps can target younger audiences. Because the screens can be programmed to respond with responsive bursts of light and sound, infants and toddlers can feel in control. Little ones have a seemingly endless desire for observing cause and effect, called *causality*. That's why they drop toys, cups, and utensils, just to watch you pick them up over and over again. Responsive apps are just one type of activity that can deliver causality. Note that you can find playthings around the home or child care environment that aren't digital and can deliver the same results, at a far lower price.

I live high up among the leaves,
and watch the farm beneath.
I love to nibble seeds and nuts -
I use my sharp front teeth.

When I'm feeling much too hot,
I find a muddy pool.
I jump right in and roll around,
until I'm nice and cool!

Axel Scheffler's Flip Flap Farm ©2015 Nosy Crow. Used with permission.

Axel Scheffler's Flip Flap Safari, by Nosy Crow (www.nosycrow.com), for iPad, ages two to five.

On the plus side: This app combines ease of use with a fun animal theme that doubles as a strong language experience. The second in the Axel Scheffler Flip Flap series (the first featured farm animals), this app follows a familiar mix-and-match play pattern, with eleven safari animals. The art is by the illustrator of *The Gruffalo*.

STAY UP TO DATE

Here's a link to CTREX reviews of the best starter apps for very young children: http://bit.ly/1KZJHaj

Need to know: The app accompanies a printed board book of the same title with easy-to-flip slit pages.

How to use it: Take turns with the toddler as you discover which animals are waiting under each page.

Doo Dah Jungle, by Doo Dah Games (https://www.facebook.com/doodahgames), for iPad, ages five and under.

On the plus side: Seven creative, fail-safe games await in Doo Dah Jungle, where a child can freely explore relationships, such as opposites, along with fine motor skills, in a risk-free setting. Tickle a gorilla to make him laugh, play dress-up with a silly giraffe, fill in the colors on jungle-themed coloring pages, and more.

Need to know: This is an excellent starter app with some fun animal surprises.

How to use it: The peekaboo games are fun to explore together.

Sago Mini Pet Cafe, by Sago Sago (www.sagosago.com), for iPad and iPhone, ages five and under.

On the plus side: Three fail-safe activities playfully pull children to a setting

Sago Mini Pet Café ©2015 Sago Sago Toys. Used with permission.

where they can discover early math and logic concepts, including counting to ten, sorting by color, matching shapes, and mixing colors. They can explore all this while doing something that every child loves—feeding animals.

Need to know: There's no way to fail, and the different animals have quirky eating behaviors, such as using a napkin or burping, to keep things interesting.

How to use it: This is a great app for taking turns feeding the hungry pets.

Sago Mini Babies, by Sago Sago (www.sagosago.com), for iPad, ages two to five.

On the plus side: This app turns your iPad into a baby-themed playground, where any tap, slap, or swipe makes something happen. Developmentally, this child-driven design technique works because toddlers start to associate their actions with the screen events. This association, in turn, builds feelings of control.

Need to know: The music-box loop can be overbearing, and you may need to show children how to find the little green arrow to get back to the main menu. These are minor points. All in all, this is a safe download with meaningful themes.

How to use it: This is a great fail-proof first app, with themes such as eating and feeding that any child will find to be meaningful.

Sago Mini Ocean Swimmer, by Sago Sago (www.sagosago.com); for Android, iPad, Kindle, and Windows; ages five and under.

Sago Mini Babies ©2015 Sago Sago Toys. Used with permission.

Sago Mini Ocean Swimmer ©2015 Sago Sago Toys. Used with permission.

On the plus side: Ocean Swimmer uses a little fish to help children explore the ocean, triggering animations that include colorful art and other characters. They can visit lots of places and there's no way to fail.

Need to know: This is the kind of app that can stimulate a lot of language, making it a nice shared experience.

How to use it: This app is excellent for guided discovery questions, such as, "I wonder what happens if you touch that mean-looking fish."

Preschoolers

If you've spent any time with three- to five-year-olds, you know they like to be in control of just about every situation, from pushing the shopping cart to figuring out where to point your garden hose. They especially like to explore as they figure things out, and one of the best tricks you can learn is how not to get between children and their interests. This is a time when they are word sponges, poised to soak up all that they find new and exciting.

Good apps use these emerging characteristics by providing a sense of accomplishment. Although children in this age range can't fluently decode, they are starting to recognize basic words, and the menus that use them, for finding content. They also know how to swipe and use the home button to get in and out of an app. This is a time of independence; they can charge the tablet on their own and organize apps into folders. Because they are egocentric at this stage, children might have trouble taking turns. It's important to offer a wide selection of apps for every possible interest area in a no-pressure setting.

Younger Preschoolers

Sago Mini Fairy Tales, by Sago Sago (www.sagosago.com); for iPad, Kindle, and Windows; ages one to five.

On the plus side: Simply touch the screen to explore thirty no-fail, animated routines inspired by popular fairy tales. This is one of a series of apps; if you like this one, you'll probably like the others. It works well as a child's first app.

How to use it: Use a guided exploration with this app in any setting (home or care center). Start it up and ask, "What happens if you touch here?"

Endless Wordplay, by Originator (www.originatorkids.com); for iPad, iPhone, iPod Touch, and Android; ages five and under.

On the plus side: A part of the Endless series, this app introduces spelling patterns and phonograms in the context of rhyming words, word puzzles, and animations that reinforce meaning. Each lesson is designed to reinforce a spelling and phonetic pattern using a sequence of rhyming word puzzles, with letters coming to life. As children play, they progressively unlock more words.

Need to know: The app features three spelling lessons with nine words that are free to try, and it has 27 additional lessons (81 words) available as an in-app purchase.

Sago Mini Fairy Tales ©2015 Sago Sago Toys. Used with permission.

My Very Hungry Caterpillar ©2015 StoryToys. Used with permission.

How to use it: More than one child can play with this app; they can play together.

My Very Hungry Caterpillar, by StoryToys (www.storytoys.com); for iPad, Windows, and Android; ages five and under.

On the plus side: Responsive and well designed, this simple virtual life simulation features Eric Carle's *The Very Hungry Caterpillar* in a way that a child can control the app.

How to use it: You can talk about the difference between pretend and real, especially when the caterpillar turns into a butterfly.

Toca Pet Doctor, by Toca Boca (http://tocaboca.com/); for iPad, Kindle, and Android; ages two to six.

On the plus side: Each of the fifteen critters in the waiting room has a problem. The worm is tangled into a knot, the cat has fleas, and the frog

Toca Pet Doctor ©2015 Toca Boca. Used with permission.

has swallowed too many flies. The cure is a fun minigame that has you swiping at flies, winding bandages, or aiming an eyedropper. After you've cured all the animals, you can wake them up to play again, but they do the same thing. The no-fail ease of use, combined with the personalities of each animal, will make this app well worth the download.

Need to know: If you like this app, you might also like Toca Doctor.

Older Preschoolers

Busy Shapes, by Edoki Academy (https://www.sevenacademy.com/en /games/discovery/busy-shapes/), for iPad, ages two to five.

On the plus side: You can't fit a round peg in a square hole, but you can have a fun time with this smart, responsive, automatically adaptive set of classification puzzles.

Busy Shapes ©2015 Edoki Academy. Used with permission.

How to use it: This is an excellent no-fail starter app.

Drive About: Number Neighborhood, by Artgig Studio (www.artgigapps.com); for iPad, iPhone, and iPod Touch; ages five and under.

Drive About: Number Neighborhood ©2015 Artgig Studio. Used with permission.

On the plus side: Children drive, fly, and sail around Number Neighborhood as they discover nine minigames that effectively reinforce school readiness skills. This is a great, no-fail download.

How to use it: Even though this app is about math, it gives children a lot to talk about, especially as they change between different vehicles. As they play, ask them to tell you what they're currently driving and where they are.

Bert loves pigeons, and pigeons love to coo.
Can you guess who Elmo loves? Elmo loves you!

Elmo Loves You! ©2015 StoryToys. Used with permission.

Elmo Loves You! by StoryToys (www.storytoys.com); for iPad, iPhone, Kindle, and Android; ages five and under.

On the plus side: Elmo Loves You! is organized around a book metaphor, with 3D pop-up pages that unfold with each swipe.

How to use it: This is a great, easy-to-use app, even if your kids aren't into Sesame Street. Don't miss the Reading Tips section of the parents' menu, with four wonderful Sesame Street video treasures on YouTube.

STAY UP TO DATE

Use the links to search through more than 300 recent, high-rated apps for children at the preschool level.

For iPad:
http://bit.ly/1NvcLfT

For Android:
http://bit.ly/1OrAlvp

Zuzu's Bananas: A Monkey Preschool Game, by Thup Games (www.thup.com); for iPad, iPhone, Android, and Kindle; ages five and under.

On the plus side: Fun, fast, and easy to play, this is a collection of fifty timed microgames, each taking no more than 15 seconds to play. The design resembles Wario Ware or Dumb Ways to Die (adapted for young children) and runs on a tablet.

Zuzu's Bananas ©2015 Thup Games. Used with permission.

How to use it: The bite-sized games make this app good for turn taking. Have children pass the tablet back and forth.

Kindergartners

Who's more nervous on the first day of kindergarten, the child or the parent? We all know the answer. Once you get over the first-day jitters, most parents will tell you the kindergarten year is a magical time for everyone involved. It's a time of new social challenges, as a child interacts with teachers and classmates and gets the chance to listen, share, take turns, and wait. Most important, it's when children learn how to spend time away from home. The kindergarten year is associated with a spurt of academic growth. Children are playing with letters and numbers, making relationships between related sounds, quantities, shapes, and sequences. The best apps for children who are in kindergarten continue the trend begun during the preschool years, providing high levels of control, lots of success, and a chance to discover both directed and open-ended activities.

Crazy Gears, by Edoki Academy (www.sevenacademy.com); for iPad, iPhone, and iPod Touch; ages six to eight.

On the plus side: This leveled, problem-solving physics game lets children freely manipulate gears, chains, rods, pulleys, and more to pull themselves to the next

Crazy Gears ©2015 Edoki Academy. Used with permission.

level. There are sixty-one puzzles, each with the same objective—to connect components and pull yourself to the next level. This is the sequel to Busy Shapes.

Need to know: There are plenty of opportunities for making mistakes (also known as debugging) to see how different mechanisms affect one another when constructing a machine.

How to use it: This app automatically moves to different levels. Visit the parents' menu to reset the level. See if you can introduce this app with your hands in your pockets.

Foos, The Hour of Code, by CodeSpark (www.codespark.org); for iPad, iPhone, iPod Touch, Kindle, and Android; ages six to eight.

On the plus side: Easy to learn and full of playful characters, this early programming experience mixes an Angry Birds type of leveling system with Scratch-style programming icons. To move your Foo character across the screen to a star, you must drag and drop the correct sequence of commands in the right order.

Snow White, by Nosy Crow (www.nosycrow.com); for iPad, iPhone, and iPod Touch; ages four to eight.

On the plus side: The masters of digital storytelling at Nosy Crow have cleverly ushered another classic fairy tale into the tablet age, with well-crafted child

I miss her smile.

Snow White ©2015 Nosy Crow. Used with permission.

narration, classical music, and detailed characters. Unlike Nosy Crow's Jack and the Beanstalk, this treatment of Snow White follows a traditional start-to-finish storyline, again told by a cast of British child-narrators. Every tap is rewarded with a proper conversational treat that changes each time. The original gender-biased, envy-driven murderous plot is more mainstream and even has a health-food twist. One of the dwarves is female, and the happy ending is sans kissing, with an ending dance scene that involves some of the same classic moves last seen in Cinderella.

Need to know: Nobody can make a story flow like Nosy Crow, which makes this app a top choice as an early language enrichment experience.

How to use it: This is a strong emergent literacy experience. Make sure children know that they can control the pace of the story and that they can pinch out to see more details in the illustrations.

Pepi Ride, by Pepiplay (www.pepiplay.com); for iPad, iPhone, iPod Touch, and Android; ages six to eight.

On the plus side: Silly, noisy, and fun, this app is ideal for graduates of Sago Road Trip. You pick out a car, decorate it, and then drive it on different tracks. The jump and speed controls can be controlled by different children, and the tracks are leveled to provide a challenge.

How to use it: Ask children to draw their car design using a pencil and paper before they start using this app. Discuss how the various parts might influence their trip.

Toca Nature, by Toca Boca (http://tocaboca.com/); for iPad, Kindle, and Android; ages six to eight.

On the plus side: Little ones can play with big ideas, such as ecosystems, as they create trees, lakes, and mountains using their fingers. A grove of oak trees spawns a deer, and a pond creates beavers and fish. Zoom in on a bear to feed it some fish, and take its photo when you are close. In addition, the entire experience provides an informal way to experiment with touch-driven two- and three-dimensional navigation tools.

Need to know: An ax icon lets you reverse mistakes. Note that the graphics are not high resolution. Scientific detail and content are lacking, and the app presents complex relationships in a general way.

Video review: http://youtu.be/2sZcGaxst7M

Toca Life: Town, by Toca Boca (http://tocaboca.com/); for iPad, iPod Touch, Android, and Kindle; ages five and under.

On the plus side: Touch, tap, and swipe your way through a small town, with six themed areas, each offering hidden surprises. As with other Toca Boca work,

Toca Life Town ©2015 Toca Boca. Used with permission.

this app is expertly crafted to ensure that children drive the app and not the other way around.

Early Elementary

Now that children this age are in school, they're much more independent with all forms of screens. It's an ideal time to expand the quantity and quality of their app library, building around their interests.

Curious Words, by Curious Hat (www.curioushat.com); for iPad, iPhone, and iPod Touch; ages six to eight.

STAY UP TO DATE

Use the link to search through more than 400 recent, high-rated apps for kindergarten-level children.

For iPad: http://bit.ly/1LSIfKu

For Android: http://bit.ly/1kdtusY

On the plus side: Easy to use and potentially powerful, this creativity video is like Vine for preschoolers. (Vine is a social network for recording video snippets, combining them into a short video, and sharing them.) In Curious Words, you are presented with a random word (such as *animal* or *fast*) and are asked to record a one second video before being prompted by the next word. The entire process is fast and easy, and the app keeps the child moving and creating. This would be a great activity for a group of children.

When all the words are recorded, they are assembled with voice-over and music, resulting in a short movie.

The random words encourage exploration, as you search for an image, pattern, color, object, or movement inspired by the word. The interface is designed to allow you to navigate to new words (swipe left or right, or double tap), change the camera filter (swipe up or down), or change the voiceover (swipe diagonally). The resulting movie can be saved to the camera roll. But don't worry; you can't save more than twelve

Curious Words ©2015 Curious Hat. Used with permission.

words per project (that's a maximum of twelve seconds). Visit http://www.curioushat.com/curious-words/ for more information.

Need to know: Swipe the word up, down, or diagonally to change the voice or camera effect.

Little Red Riding Hood, by Nosy Crow (www.nosycrow.com); for iPad, iPhone, and iPod Touch; ages six to eight.

On the plus side: See the video at http://youtu.be/emR8_vqJdlQ

This funny, easy-to-control edition of Little Red Riding Hood is full of surprises, including an ending that you help create. You can take eight paths through the woods, where you collect various items you'll need to trick the wolf and free Grandma from the closet. This is one of the most notable accomplishments from British-based Nosy Crow to date.

Need to know: You may recall that the traditional version of this tale has a rather gory theme of being eaten by a wolf. This time, the wolf locks Grandma in a closet, and depending on which items you collect, is scared away by a spider or conquered in some other way.

Montessori Math City, by Edoki by Les Trois Elles (http://edoki.net/); for iPad, iPhone, and Android; ages five to ten.

On the plus side: This app is ideal for helping an older preschooler or kindergarten-age child better understand base-ten numbers. French-based Les Trois Elles Interactive continues the tradition of giving children the tools they need to build their understanding of the way numbers work.

There are two modes of play, both inspired directly by traditional Montessori materials. Golden Beads lets children first complete a units board, one bead at a time, up to 1,000. Number Blocks challenges children to build a target number, by dragging the correct ones, tens, hundreds, or thousands blocks into place. Correct answers are rewarded with more buildings that you can drag and drop onto your city. Progress is bookmarked automatically, so you can come back and do more later. Profiles can be saved for multiple children, increasing the usefulness for classrooms.

Need to know: Children should have the prerequisite ability to count to ten before using this app. If you're looking for a game element, you won't find it in this app.

MyBackpack, by Waterford Institute (www.waterford.org), for iPad, ages three and up.

On the plus side: Looking for an educational bargain? Download this app. You can't argue with the price of this set of e-books, math drills, movies, and nursery rhymes—free.

Adapted for tablets from Waterford's school curriculum, this is a nice collection of no-strings-attached content.

Although the books are clunky, they offer touch-and-hear scaffolding and sixteen popular stories.

There are four leveled math drills that serve up twenty-five progressive levels by way of four games: Balloon Race, Rock Climb, Let's Build, and Frustration! Each has you helping an animal get to a goal by solving math-fact problems as quickly as possible. In Frustration, you try to beat your own time.

Other features include thirty-five original songs designed to illustrate reading, math, and science concepts, and five nursery rhyme read-alongs presented in board book format. From an interactive point of view, the stories are limited. But they are solid stories, and children can choose to listen to them if they would like.

Need to know: The math games shine, but the e-books are not as great.

TeleStory, by Launchpad Toys (http://launchpadtoys.com); for iPad, iPhone, and iPod Touch; ages six to eight.

On the plus side: Turn your iPad into a TV studio where you're the star. The process is simple, thanks to auto-props that use face recognition to automatically provide props and wardrobe items. You start by choosing from four themes: the news, a music video, taking a drive as a private eye, and a Star Wars–like theme. Next, you can mix and match from over thirty animated scenes, recording yourself as the central character. The content includes fifty digital costume items, each with face-tracking abilities; these items include glasses, wigs, hands, and so on.

Need to know: You have to create a parent account to share projects online, which requires email verification. I did not see any worrisome content.

Thinkrolls 2, by Avokiddo (www .avokiddo.com); for iPad, iPhone, iPod Touch, Android, and Amazon Fire; ages three to nine.

On the plus side: Swipe your way through a series of increasingly challenging mazes in this second edition of Thinkrolls, the well-named series that gently

Thinkrolls 2 ©2015 Avokiddo. Used with permission.

introduces properties of matter and physics. You quickly discover that the Thinkrolls can do more than roll—they float, glide, and teleport through the themed chapters.

Need to know: Each chapter gradually introduces a new scientific concept: Accordion presents fine motor skills as children use expansion and compression to open pathways, build bridges, and create stairways. Water and Barrel deals with sinking or floating. Egg presents force, acceleration, and gravity. Fan contains aerodynamic concepts and fans. Wormhole asks you to use coordinates to get back. Battery deals with electrical and circuits. Light bulb contains visual memory challenges. There are 117 easy levels for ages three to five and 118 hard levels for ages five to nine. Features include the ability to track progress for up to six player profiles. All in all, this is an outstanding collection of challenges.

How to use it: Make sure you start at the easiest level. Once you get the ball rolling with this app, just sit back and observe. If a child gets stuck, point and ask, "What do you think will happen if you move the barrel over here?"

Toca Kitchen 2, by Toca Boca (http://tocaboca.com/); for iPad, iPhone, Kindle, Windows, and Android; ages three to eight.

On the plus side: It's always nice to see a good app get better. If you liked the first Toca Kitchen, then you'll like this update. Although the play pattern and

Toca Kitchen 2 ©2015 Toca Boca. Used with permission.

the content are about the same, you can now do more with the food items you have. There's a set of food storage trays, so you can mix and match food items and a salt and pepper shaker. The content includes fourteen ingredients (mostly the same as the previous version of the game). If you're looking for manners when eating, this isn't your app. Multitouch features make it possible for two children to collaborate. This app is nicely free of licensed content and purchase links.

Need to know: Explore your tablet's settings menu to turn meat items on or off. You can also adjust sound and turn off the Toca Boca store icon.

How to use it: This is great social play. Take turns dragging items into the frying pan. This can be a rich language experience, giving children a lot to talk about.

Video review: http://youtu.be/8d1G7Kbpuqc

Understanding Math—Addition and Subtraction, by Appp Media (www.apppmedia.com), for iPad, ages six to eight.

On the plus side: Features include unlimited user profiles (children must enter their name) and the ability to track each child's achievements by both quality (accuracy) and quantity, and the ability to see how to add and subtract quantities of up to 100 in four different settings. Because the numbers change in real time, children can start making associations between objects and symbols. A dual mode lets two children compete at once for three of the activities.

Need to know: If you're looking for bells and whistles, you won't find it with this app. Take note of the excellent record-keeping system for an unlimited number of children.

Water Bears, by Schell Games (http://schellgames.com), for iPad and Android, ages four and up.

On the plus side: Here's a well-designed 3D pipe puzzle that takes advantage of the iPad's slippery screen to serve up fifty puzzles, arranged from easy to hard. The goal in each puzzle is the same: to

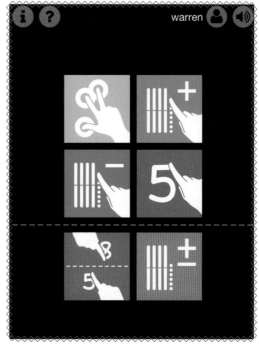

Understanding Math—Addition and Subtraction
©2015 Appp Media. Used with permission.

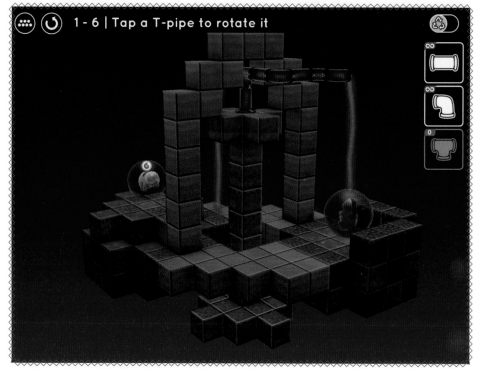

Water Bears ©2015 Schell Games. Used with permission.

deliver the colored water to the associated blob-like water bears. You do this by dragging and dropping pipe sections into place.

Need to know: It would be helpful to have a more obvious hint system on some of the levels and a better undo feature. In all, though, this game is easy to learn, and the interface can be used by younger children, despite some required reading skills. Full control over game sounds is given, increasing classroom appeal.

How to use it: Two children can play this app together to solve puzzles, which creates a structured, collaborative problem-solving experience.

Video review: https://youtu.be/PqkPinJBzn4

Winky Think Logic Puzzles, by Spinlight Studio (http://spinlight.com/), for iPad, ages six to eight.

On the plus side: Simplicity meets complexity in this collection of 180 bite-sized logic puzzles.

The first level begins quickly with no introduction, and the familiar type of leveling menu (similar to Angry Birds) makes it easy to choose a level. To start, you drag a shape to a target as quickly as you can (also see Busy Shapes for a similar design). This unlocks level 2, which is a bit harder. The

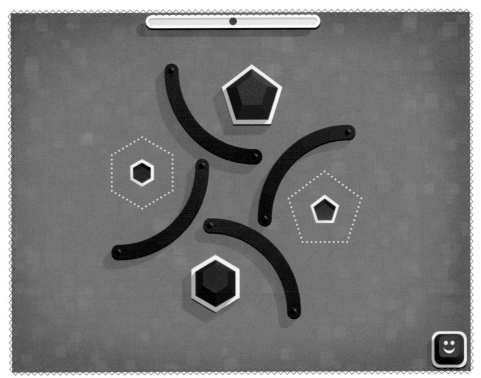

Winky Think Logic Puzzles ©2015 Spinlight Studio. Used with permission.

level-select menu is innovative but unconventional, which takes some getting used to.

Once you've solved a level, you can go back to a previous challenge; but you can't jump ahead. The background music is well designed, can be toggled on or off, and doesn't get in the way of the game sounds. There is no language prerequisite. The only thing missing is a hint system. Some of the puzzles use multitouch features, which require two fingers (or players) working cooperatively to solve a puzzle. Some puzzles require using simple machines and chain reactions. The bottom line? This is an extremely exciting logic challenge.

Need to know: Note that this is a Sprang app, which promotes additional apps by way of in-app advertising. In this case, additional apps are promoted on the level-select menu, and the age-gating system is not appropriate considering the challenge presented by this app.

STAY UP TO DATE

Use the links to search through more than 400 recent, high-rated apps for early elementary children.

For iPad:
http://bit.ly/1MfhHBg

For Android:
http://bit.ly/1RZhQMA

Apps by Subject

It's amazing to think that today we can hand a child a single device that costs less than a bicycle and serves as a direct connection to every scientific or artistic breakthrough ever made. But such power comes with responsibility and requires the ability to match the right software and hardware with the child.

Start with what you know about each child. Ask, "How can this particular program help this individual child learn?" In the early stages, you will need to do a lot of observing how the child uses the tablet and the app and then keep tweaking your choices. An app that gets a high rating from an adult might get a thumbs-down from a child. Meanwhile, the child might play on a friend's tablet and become obsessed with an app that is unfamiliar to you. It is important to understand the children, know about each child's interests and learning challenges, think about what the app can teach the child, and choose appropriately for the school or home setting.

When evaluating interactive products for children, keep in mind the following aspects:

- **Easy usage**—Children should have a feeling of success in the first few seconds; reversibility and hooks of meaning that work with the intended audience are also helpful. The interface is crisp and responsive with no lags or moments in which the user cries out for help.

- **Entertaining**—The experience should be fun. Besides being easy to use, the app should be designed with appropriate levels, a degree of novelty, and a good story.

- **Educational**—Ideally, a child will walk away from the app with something new and valuable. Educational value can be enhanced by tutorial elements—sometimes called scaffolds—that offer assistance at just the right time.

- **Features**—The ability to customize the interface to the child, adjust background music, swap language, and track progress all tie into the final rating of an app. But it is important to consider these features in the context of the other factors being considered.

- **Overall value**—When all things are considered, including the current state of the app, how much does this experience cost versus what it can do?

With all those considerations in mind, I have provided a sampling of app recommendations for some of the more common subject areas.

Astronomy

Make the night skies come to life with these apps.

Star Walk Kids—Explore Space and Planets, by Vito Technology (www.vitotechnology.com); for iPad, iPhone, iPod Touch, and Android; ages six to eight.

On the plus side: One of my favorite astronomy apps, Star Walk, now has a nicely designed children's version with hand-drawn graphics. Despite the child-friendly look and pared-back content, the features that made the original Star Walk amazing still work with this app—namely, the ability to point your device at the sky to identify a star, constellation, or planet. The app uses your built-in gyroscope to match the map on your screen to the stars seen from your location.

Need to know: Those looking for comprehensive content need to look elsewhere. This app only deals with ten planets, seventeen stars, forty-three constellations, and two satellites (the Hubble Space Telescope and the International Space Station). It also offers six short movies that are well done.

Solar System for iPad, by Touch Press (www.touchpress.com), for iPad, ages six and up.

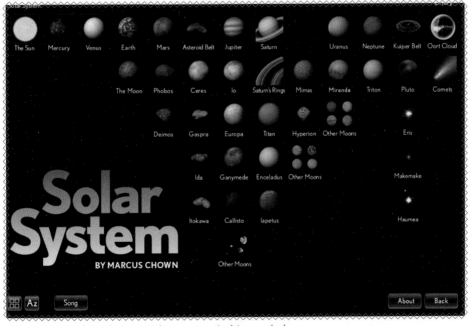

Solar System for iPad ©2015 Touchpress. Used with permission.

On the plus side: In this carefully crafted interactive science poster, touch a planet, moon, or comet to explore different aspects of our solar system. Point out the location-based slider on the screen bottom, which starts with the center of the solar system (the sun) and moves out to the distant comets. This space-line serves as a constant table of contents, helping you to jump around quickly through huge distances.

Need to know: This app is pricier than many others, but users love the graphics.

How to use it: Let children play with the working model of the solar system, which lets them zoom in or out on the model and allows them to swipe to adjust units of time or their view in the system.

Drawing and Coloring

Tablets will never replace the feeling of dipping your fingers in gooey, bright paint and spreading it on paper, but they can offer children new ways to create art and experiment.

5 Fingers Paint, by Blue Peak Mobile; for iPad, iPhone, and iPod Touch; up to age five.

On the plus side: This simple yet powerful app turns the iPad's multitouch screen into a messy, creative space, where every finger has a job. You get five colors

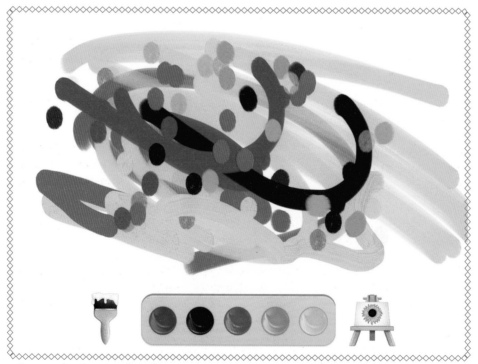

5 Fingers Paint. ©2015 Uroš Katić. Used with permission.

(one per finger) and nice, thick lines. The colors seem to smear into one another, and faster motions result in faded lines. These features give you the feeling that you are using real paint. Twitter and Facebook features are age-gated.

Need to know: The screen-clearing mechanism is innovative but potentially confusing to younger children. Also, a more straightforward main menu would be helpful. Finally, in the iPad's Settings, under General, you will need to turn off Multitasking Gestures.

Video review: http://youtu.be/jwtKO6HVAaw

Bubl Draw, by Bubl (www.bublbubl.com), for iPad, ages one to seven.

On the plus side: Convert your iPad into a colorful, musical easel, where any touch makes something happen. After you make a doodle, you can tap any line a second time to generate a rhythmic pattern. A set of tools lets you change musical styles. Need to know: Things happen randomly, so it's easy to quickly clutter the screen. Show children how to clear the screen.

Quiver (formerly called ColAR Mix), by Puteko Limited (http://quivervision .com/); for iPad, iPhone, and Android; ages six to eight.

On the plus side: Coloring pages have been around for decades, and augmented reality has been around for years. But it took an app and some black-line PDFs that you can download from the Quiver website (http://quivervision.com/) to bring them together. First released in 2014 under the name ColAR Mix in New Zealand, this app brings black-line coloring pages to life. When you open the app and use your device's camera to view the page you have colored, animated images appear. Children can watch their images from any angle, play or pause their animations, and zoom in for a closer look.

Need to know: This app doesn't work on older iOS devices (iPod and iPhone3 or earlier).

Four sheets come free; eight are sold for $2.99 as an in-app sale. To print out pages, visit http://quivervision.com/. The locked pages are shown to children, which could tempt them into making an in-app purchase. In-app options include a dot template from author Peter Reynolds.

Draw and Tell HD, by Duck Duck Moose Design (www.duckduckmoose.com), for iPad and Android, ages five and under.

On the plus side: As with apps like Doodlecast, this app turns your tablet into a magical flannel board, with elements that can be narrated as they are highlighted on the screen. There's a nice variety of stickers, colors, and drawing tools.

Need to know: The visual tools combined with the narration option make this a strong language experience.

OverColor, by Popapp Factory (www.popappfactory.com), for iPad, ages six and up.

On the plus side: Ready to twist up your thinking? This clever visual brainteaser asks you to copy a model using a set of geometric overlays. They start easy and get hard.

Need to know: The one hundred puzzles and the first levels are pretty easy. There's no time pressure, but there are also no hints or game elements.

How to use it: Play this app together with the child.

Cars and Trucks

Children in the early years are fascinated with cars and trucks and driving. Thanks to the motion sensors inside tablets called accelerometers, children can actually use their tablets like steering wheels. The following selections foster fine motor control, providing a setting for social play.

Auto Repair, by 5baam (http://5baam.com/), for iPad, ages five and under.

On the plus side: Twenty-one problems are waiting to be fixed in four zany cars designed with typical boy and girl themes. There's a lot of sorting, connecting wires of the same color, connecting circuits, patching leaks, and so on. Each time children solve a problem, they earn a badge that is saved over time. After you choose a car, you see the problems for each, highlighted. Innovative features include tilting the screen to pour the oil and turning your screen upside down to look under a car on the lift.

This is a fast, fun, irreverent app with some hidden surprises that encourage frequent visits. Some of the underlying concepts include connecting paths to complete circuits, learning about oil and pistons, replacing windshield glass, and so on. The app offers different difficulty levels and does not track high scores. When all the activities are complete, the child can start over. According to the publisher, there are no in-app purchases.

Labo Car Designer, by Labo Lado Inc. (www.labolado.com), for iPad and Android, ages three to five.

On the plus side: Sketching and drawing programs are easy to find, but this one lets you draw something that many children find fascinating: cars. Drawing and driving are two parts to this app.

To design a car, you can either start with a blank page (and two wheels) or choose from twenty-seven themed templates. Once your car is designed, you can take it for a drive on the virtual road with plenty of bumps and bridges. As you drive, you can toggle between weather situations and between night and day.

Need to know: The car is fun to drive, but it does not offer a lot of controls other than forward, backward, and hop.

Labo Car Designer ©2015 Labo Lado. Used with permission.

More Trucks HD, by Duck Duck Moose Inc. (http://www.duckduckmoose.com/); for iPhone, iPad, and Android; ages three to five.

On the plus side: This sequel to the first Trucks from Duck Duck Moose offers fun and playful vehicle-themed activities. Children can put out fires, play tic-tac-toe against the firehouse dog, and have drag races.

Need to know: Girls should not be put off by the big-truck theme. The play patterns used in driving this app will appeal to both genders and all ages. Some of the activities are tricky at first, so be on hand to provide help the first time through.

Video review: http://youtu.be/aQhmzWyggM4

Toca Cars, by Toca Boca (http://tocaboca.com/); for iPad, iPhone, and Android; ages three to nine.

On the plus side: The cars follow your finger, which makes them hard to control but adds to the fun. The result is a compelling fine motor experience that's easy for children to fool around with and explore, but then they'll still be playing an hour later. Don't overlook the dog that chases the car. There are no rules and lots of possibilities.

Toca Cars ©2015 Toca Boca. Used with permission.

Need to know: It would be helpful to have a larger area to explore (the driving area seems similar to the area found in Toca Builders). As noted, the cars are not so easy to control. This is one of the most innovative Toca Boca apps.

Pepi Ride, by Pepiplay (www.pepiplay.com); for iPad, iPhone, iPod Touch, and Android; ages six to eight.

On the plus side: Silly, noisy, and fun, this app is ideal for the graduates of Sago Road Trip. You pick out a car, decorate it, and then drive it on different tracks. The jump and speed controls can be controlled by different children, and the tracks are leveled to provide a challenge. However, a child always has a choice to stay on an easier level.

The adventure begins in the garage, where you choose a car, give it a paint job, and accessorize with a horn or a rocket pack. As you drive, you unlock new tracks, from nine available. There's a nice variety of challenges, from a sunny beach with simple hills to stumps, tree ropes, footbridges, and rocks.

In English, Czech, Dutch, French, German, Italian, Japanese, Korean, Polish, Portuguese, Russian, Simplified Chinese, Spanish, Swedish, Traditional Chinese, and Turkish.

Need to know: Sadly, you can't turn down the repetitive background music.

Geography

By using these apps, children can view their local environment from a new perspective when they put down their devices, go outside, and look at the world around them.

Geocaching, by Groundspeak (www.groundspeak.com), for iPad or Android, ages six and up.

On the plus side: Technology meets fresh air and sunshine, with a generous dose of deductive reasoning, persistence, and map reading—all in the form of geocaching. The treasures (called geocaches) can vary widely in size and sophistication. They may be as small as a magnetic key box containing a tiny scroll of paper or as large as a waterproof ammo box that is stuffed into a tree hole.

To find a geocache, you need a computer and a GPS, or better yet, a smartphone loaded with the app. Groundspeak makes money by selling the app and a variety of geocache supplies.

Need to know: The free version of the app, called Geocaching Intro, forces you to create an account. It has nearly all the functionality of the $9.99 premium app but doesn't list all the geocaches.

Google Earth and **Google Maps,** by Google Inc. (www.google.com); for Windows, iPad, iPhone, Android, and Chrome; ages seven and up.

On the plus side: One single free app puts any location at your fingertips with exciting new features such as Street View, 3D buildings, and much more. It is a stellar example of how interactive media can make abstract geographical and spatial concepts leap out. Younger children can get a sense of how their neighborhood fits into their town, their county, their state, and their continent. Other education applications are numerous—for mapping and geography, as well as for other more indirect uses, including science, history, and math.

Need to know: You'll need a good Internet connection.

World Landmarks Explorer, by Peapod Labs (www.peapodlabs.com), for iPad, ages four and up.

On the plus side: Here's a good way to bring geography to life. Good for all ages, including adults, this program contains the same swipe-and-explore navigation used in the ABC Explorer apps. But there's a new twist; it offers satellite views of 112 world landmarks from 53 countries by way of Google Maps. When combined with YouTube videos and 336 jaw-dropping photos, this app puts a lot of wow at your fingertips.

Need to know: No reading is required, which is both a strength and a weakness. The addition of short paragraphs would increase the language enrichment value

World Landmarks Explorer ©2015 Peapod Labs. Used with permission.

of this app. It would also be useful to have the option to turn off the looping background music.

Handwriting

Let's hope that good penmanship will never die, in part because we'll always need good fine motor skills to use tablets.

Cursive Writing Wizard—Trace Letters and Words, by L'Escapadou (http://lescapadou.com), for iPad and Android, ages six to eight.

On the plus side: Turn your tablet into a highly customizable cursive writing tutorial that takes up where Writing Wizard has left off. The best part about this app is the way you can customize it to just about any child or school curriculum.

Need to know: Teachers take note that your conception of how a child learns to write cursive letters just might change. Parents take note that your kindergartner can come to school knowing cursive. Available in D'Nealian, Zaner-Bloser, and two French fonts.

Horses

Lars and Friends, by Carla Susanto (http://larsandfriends.com), for iPad and Android, ages five and under.

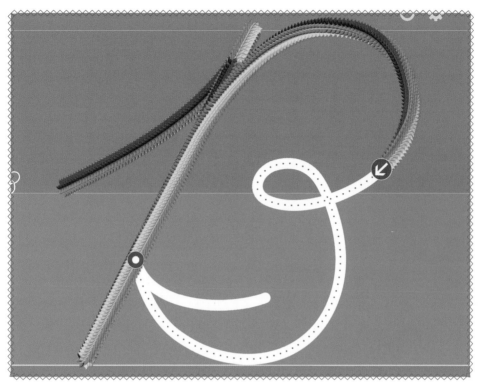

Cursive Writing Wizard ©2015 L'Escapadou. Used with permission.

On the plus side: Beautiful horse-related illustrations are mixed with limited interactive design in this story app by Brooklyn-based artist Carla Susanto. In the story, children explore fantasy worlds with a horse named Lars.

Need to know: The narration is fair, with no text scaffolding features (but you can hear the text read out loud). But the spring-loaded animated hot spots seem rather random and do little to support the narrative. Weaknesses include page-turning buttons that are too small on an iPad Mini and are sometimes unresponsive. Additional content includes a drag-and-drop jigsaw puzzle game.

Languages Other than English

Many apps let children toggle between languages. If you let them experiment, they can build familiarity with common words in different languages, such as Spanish or Chinese.

ABC Actions, by Peapod Labs (www.peapodlabs.com); for iPad, iPhone, and iPod Touch; ages five and under.

On the plus side: Fifty common action words—in English or Spanish—come to life through 150 clear, authentic, open-source photos and one hundred select videos from YouTube.

ABC Actions ©2015 Peapod Labs. Used with permission.

This is an easy-to-use, richly illustrated language experience that can gently introduce either English or Spanish vocabulary. Especially helpful is the ability to toggle between Spanish or English on the fly.

Need to know: Note that you need an Internet connection to view the YouTube content; when offline, the videos don't play. It is important to update this app frequently to keep the YouTube links working.

Spanish Stagecraft, by Playmation Studios Inc. (http://playmationstudios.com); for iPad, iPhone, and iPod Touch; for ages six and up.

On the plus side: If children want to learn Spanish, they can build their own sentences by freely manipulating sentence parts. The visual scaffolds make it all possible.

The child might see and hear a sentence such as "La mujer cierra la ventana," with five items shown on the bottom of the screen. When the child drags and drops the correct items (a woman and an open window), a draft sentence describes what he is doing in real time.

Need to know: The main menu is confusing, the background music is bothersome, and the voice quality is grainy. This program also has in-app sales. Despite these shortcomings, this is an innovative app with useful capabilities.

El hombre lee el diario.

Spanish Stagecraft ©2015 Playmation Studios. Used with permission.

Video demo: http://bit.ly/1JHNCv5

Listening and Auditory Discrimination

Children can have fun while stretching their speaking and listening skills with this noteworthy app.

SmackTalk Kids 1.3, by Marcus Satellite (www.marcussatellite.com); for iPad, iPhone, and iPod Touch with external microphone; ages three and up.

On the plus side: This is an echo chamber app, similar to Talking Tom. See your voice coming out of a kitten, dog, chihuahua, or guinea pig. You say a short phrase, such as "have a nice day" and see your voice coming out of an animal, nearly perfectly lip-synced. Once your voice is recorded, you can modify the pitch, pacing, and so on. New features include a Kid Mode to lock advanced features, the ability to route the audio to the external speakers, better control over the voice triggers, and a set of sliders to change the pitch. You can find other versions of this type of app, but this one works well and offers many features.

Math and Logic

Whether you want children to have practice counting or comparing quantities, you can find many good apps that support early mathematical learning.

Montessori Math City, by Edoki by Les Trois Elles Interactive (http://edoki.net); for iPad, iPhone, and Android; ages five to ten.

On the plus side: This app by Les Trois Elles Interactive continues the tradition of giving children the tools they need to build early math understanding. There are two modes of play, both inspired directly by traditional Montessori materials. In each, you build target numbers by dragging blocks in units of ones, tens, hundreds, or thousands into place. Feedback is provided instantly, and you can earn points to build your own city (hence the name).

Need to know: Children should have the prerequisite ability to count to ten before using this app. There's not much of a game element.

Video review: http://youtu.be/xN-lcCKtung

Slice Fractions, by Ululab Inc. (http://ululab.com); for iPad, iPhone, iPod Touch, and Android; ages six to eight.

On the plus side: This app was already a favorite and is getting even better. Since August 2014, thirty-two additional levels have been added as an update (at no extra cost), plus the app offers a new underground world with singing mushrooms.

Quick Math Jr., by Shiny Things (www.getshinythings.com), for iPad and iPhone, ages five and under.

Slice Fractions ©2015 Ululab. Used with permission.

On the plus side: Responsive, playful, and adaptive, this early math experience contains developmentally appropriate math problem-solving opportunities that make it an excellent addition to any school or home tablet. Children count to one hundred; connect number names, numerals, and quantities up to thirty (including zero); and quickly count groups using small collections of objects in dice patterns, ten-frames, and random patterns.

How to use it: This app is easy to match with your school's math curriculum.

Music

You can easily find apps that let children explore making music, use modified synthesizers, and learn skills such as notation.

Auxy Music Creation, by Auxy (www.auxy.co), for iPad, ages eight and up.

On the plus side: You can turn your tablet into a music machine with this easy-to-use music editor. New features (on Version 1.2.1) include paid add-ons, such as the ability to export your work as a MIDI file. This free app lets you do a lot, and the in-app purchases are not imposing.

Note that it is possible to set the velocity for individual notes, or draw triplets or 1/32 notes.

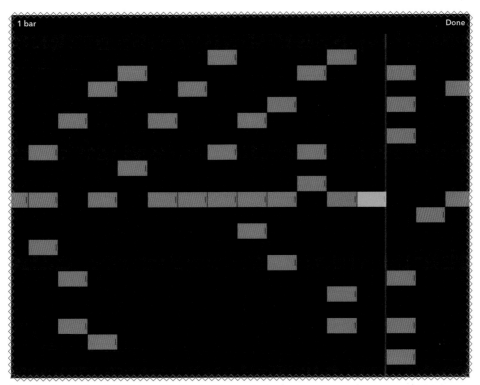

Auxy Music Creation ©2015 Auxy AB. Used with permission.

Need to know: Despite the simple interface, this app has a lot of depth. Use guided discovery to help children find hidden features.

How to use it: This app makes it easy to see the math relationships in music (each measure is 1/8). Children will need a bit of guided discovery to get started with this app.

Video demo: http://youtu.be/fw2xjfzYc8U

Reading Experiences

Now you can find quality children's literature on tablet screens, but don't worry—e-books are no threat to traditional books. It actually makes little sense to compare the two types because the behaviors of parents and children when reading them are so different. Reading print books tends to involve more parent-child conversations about the content, which is good! But e-books can become a nice way to extend the narrative of a story into additional types of play.

Cat in the Hat—Read & Learn—Dr. Seuss, by Oceanhouse Media (www .oceanhousemedia.com); for iPad, iPhone, and iPod Touch; ages three to five.

On the plus side: The first part of a new series called Read and Learn from Oceanhouse Media, this app layers new features onto the original Cat in the Hat

Cat in the Hat—Read & Learn—Dr. Seuss ©2015 Oceanhouse Media. Used with permission.

art and narration, with options that let you tell the original story, if you would like. Animated features respond to a child without interrupting the story. The rain in the window always follows the angle of the screen, for example, and a hidden star on each page can launch a short challenge related to the story.

Need to know: The only downside? The higher price (about $4.99). But for this level of quality, it's worth it.

Video demo: https://youtu.be/zku7LpanVUg

Petting Zoo, by Fox and Sheep (http://www.foxandsheep.com/), for iPad and Android, ages three and up.

On the plus side: Ideal for big screens, this innovative set of twenty-one animal-related sketches by Christoph Niemann (a cartoonist for the *New York Times*) uses animation to morph one image into another. As a bonus, you can interact with the images by touching the screen. You can help fish turn inside out and snakes turn into jump ropes.

Need to know: Because the format never changes, a child's interest may fade once the novelty wears off.

Where's My Monster? by Martin Hughes (https://itunes.apple.com/us/app /wheres-my-monster/id826050780?mt=8); for iPad, iPhone, iPod Touch, and Android; ages five and under.

On the plus side: Thirteen monsters are hiding behind red pull tabs in this clever story about a mother trying to find her child. Children can read the text or click to have it read aloud. They can pull to open the door, drawers, and closet, and can check many more hiding places before finding Mother's Monster.

Need to know: Just thirteen monsters are available to find. All in all, this is an excellent app for children as young as three, and it makes a nice language enrichment app as well.

Little Red Riding Hood, by Nosy Crow (www.nosycrow.com); for iPad, iPhone, and iPod Touch; ages six to eight.

On the plus side: This funny, easy-to-control edition of Little Red Riding Hood is full of surprises, including an ending that you help create. You can take eight paths through the woods, where you collect various items you'll need to trick the wolf and free Grandma from the closet. This is one of the most notable accomplishments from British-based Nosy Crow to date.

Need to know: You may recall that the traditional version of this tale has a rather gory theme of being eaten by a wolf. This time, the wolf locks Grandma in a closet. Depending on which items you collect, you might see a spider scare the wolf away.

Video review: http://youtu.be/emR8_vqJdlQ

Reading Skills

Here are some apps that can turn your tablet into a patient reading tutor that adjusts levels according to your child's ability. Skills supported range from letter recognition to comprehension.

Endless Reader, by Originator (www.originatorkids.com), for iPad or iPhone, ages three to seven.

On the plus side: Ninety-nine common sight words extend Originator's first app, Endless Alphabet. This time, you build words first and then place them inside sentences. The words come to life the instant they find their home. The best part is that all the dragging and dropping can be shared by more than one child. Level 1 is for pre-K through kindergarten, Level 2 is for early elementary, and Level 3 covers middle elementary.

Need to know: The free version of the app teases you with a set of starter words. You have to pay about $5 for an additional pack of 20 words or about $12 for all 99 words.

The Joy of Reading, by Edoki Academy (www.sevenacademy.com); for iPad, iPhone, iPod Touch, and Android; for ages three to six.

Joy of Reading ©2015 Edoki Academy. Used with permission.

On the plus side: Priced for home use but containing features that qualify it for classrooms, The Joy of Reading combines robust record-keeping features with a playful set of structured reading activities.

The curriculum comes from Robert Savage of McGill University and Françoise Boulanger, a reading teacher. Content includes eight games designed to provide drill and practice recognizing words on labels, rhyming, tracing uppercase and lowercase letters, and recognizing consonant sounds and long vowels in the context of significant words, such as the child's own first name. The app comes with 3,000 first names, and the user can add others.

The app adds fundamental vocabulary-building words as the child progresses, and adults can record and copy an unlimited number of words to support the learning journey.

Need to know: The web-based Parental Dashboard lets parents and educators create up to forty profiles for tracking children's progress.

Video review: http://youtu.be/H9NvvfSQiXM

MyBackpack, by Waterford Institute (www.waterford.org), for iPad, ages three and up.

On the plus side: Adapted for tablet from Waterford's school curriculum, this is a nice collection of no-strings-attached content. This free app provides a set of e-books, math drills, movies, and nursery rhymes.

Although the books are clunky, they offer touch-and-hear scaffolding for 16 popular stories. Four leveled math drills serve up twenty-five progressive levels by way of four games: Balloon Race, Rock Climb, Let's Build, and Frustration! Each has you helping an animal get to a goal by solving math fact problems as quickly as possible. In Frustration, you try to beat your own time.

Other features include thirty-five original songs designed to illustrate reading, math, and science concepts, and five nursery rhyme read-alongs presented in board-book format. From an interactive point of view, the stories are limited but solid, and children can choose to listen to them if they would like.

Need to know: The math games shine; the e-books are not as polished. But you can't argue with the price.

Word Wizard, by L'Escapadou (http://lescapadou.com), for iPad and iPhone, ages four to ten.

On the plus side: Turn your tablet into a talking alphabet and language generator; it is the perfect tool for a child just starting to experiment with letters and sounds. To build a word, you drag it from an alphabet strip onto a letter grid, where it snaps into place, pronouncing any word that might be created, including nonsense words.

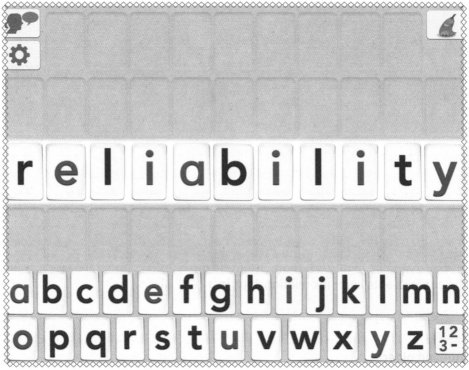

Word Wizard ©2015 L'Escapadou. Used with permission.

Need to know: This is an open-ended language-creation tool, so a child could potentially spell swear words.

Video demo: http://youtu.be/8fYgd8f1xiM

Science

Whether it's horses, hamsters, dinosaurs, or rockets, young children have no shortage of questions. A search engine such as Bing or Google is the ideal source of answers, as long as you're by their side to model how to type in the search criteria. As children grow, they will develop strong passions for interests that may influence how they turn out as adults. Now a child can see inside a submarine, explore a human heart, or sit inside an Apollo space capsule.

The Human Body, by Tinybop (www.tinybop.com); for iPad, iPhone, and iPod Touch; ages three and up.

On the plus side: We all wonder how our bodies work. This app helps answer all those endless questions and hard-to-understand concepts such as "How does my heart work?" and "How many bones do I have?" The animated graphics are clear of embarrassing images and free of gore. Don't miss the interactive features found in the eye, heart, and ear, which incorporate features of a camera and a microphone.

Need to know: This app can store individual profiles for each child. You can also hide recorded messages inside the graphics.

How to use it: You can customize this app for a child's reading level. You can also embed your own voice tags inside the app, helping children own this experience.

Toca Nature, by Toca Boca (http://tocaboca.com/); for iPad, Kindle, and Android; ages six to eight.

On the plus side: Little ones can play with big ideas, such as ecosystems, as they create trees, lakes, and mountains using their fingers. A grove of oak trees spawns a deer, and a pond creates beavers and fish. The child can zoom in on a bear to feed it some fish and take its photo up close. In addition, the entire experience provides an informal way to experiment with touch-driven two- and three-dimensional navigation tools.

Need to know: An ax icon lets children reverse their mistakes. Note that the graphics are not high resolution. Scientific detail and content are lacking, and the app presents complex relationships in a general way.

Video review: http://youtu.be/2sZcGaxst7M

The Earth, by Tinybop (www.tinybop.com); for iPad, iPhone, and iPod Touch; ages four and older.

Toca Nature ©2015 Toca Boca. Used with permission.

On the plus side: Our planet is always changing, right under our feet. But how do you make these big, abstract concepts meaningful to a curious young child? Here's the perfect app. The fifth in Tinybop's Explorer's Library series is also one of the best (we also highly recommend the Human Body). You start with a translucent model of the earth that spins with a swipe. The child can cut it in half with a cross-section tool and can also use a geological timeline to envision how the Earth would have looked when it was first forming. As with the other Tinybop apps, the child's finger drives the concepts, not the other way around.

The good stuff happens when the child zooms in to a detailed depiction of our planet's surface and touches one of twelve magnifying glasses or windows that zoom into a detailed scene. Many scenes let the child drive a specific process. Children can change the shape and height of the volcano in real time and tap the lava to make it erupt. They can make ice form in crevices to make a rock fall or launch an iceberg by making waves. Other nice touches include a vocabulary feature with drag-and-drop labels and a detailed PDF user manual that helps you better understand each process.

The distinctive illustrations are by Sarah Jacoby. Vocabulary is in more than forty languages with interactive labels. The bottom line? This is a great way to let children playfully discover some of the big ideas they'll encounter later on in their school curriculum.

Rounds: Franklin Frog ©2015 Nosy Crow. Used with permission.

Need to know: Teachers, don't overlook the PDF handbook designed to support learning.

Video review: https://youtu.be/TcGP-92FtEk

Rounds: Franklin Frog, by Nosy Crow (www.nosycrow.com); for iPad, iPhone, and iPod Touch; ages four to eight.

On the plus side: This innovative app stretches the definition of an e-book, with a dash of Nosy Crow irreverence.

Franklin Frog is the first title in a series of nonfiction apps that deal with life cycles.

Need to know: The background music is extremely well done, but you can't turn it off or separate it from the narration or other sounds. This critique is more relevant for classroom settings.

MarcoPolo Ocean, by MarcoPolo Learning Inc. (http://gomarcopolo.com), for iPad, ages three and up.

On the plus side: Hundreds of ocean-related items can be arranged on the screen in this set of interactive puzzles. Each item comes with a short description that is narrated by a marine biologist.

MarcoPolo Ocean ©2015 MarcoPolo Learning. Used with permission.

This sandbox-style app lets children construct knowledge about oceans by interacting with one fish, shell, or boat at a time.

Need to know: Visit the parents' menu, where you can toggle on and off the tropical background music and adjust the level of factual information. You can also reset the child's ocean, if necessary.

How to use it: This is an outstanding way to build a child's emerging interest in oceanography without ever getting wet feet.

Video preview: http://vimeo.com/81442324

Journeys of Invention, by Touchpress Ltd. (http://journeysofinvention.com/), for iPad, ages six and up.

On the plus side: Turn your tablet into a science museum, full of historical items that invite exploration. Children can see one of the first Apple 1 computers, the Apollo 10 command module, and seventy-eight additional historical artifacts of invention. Each is presented via crisp, clear photography and 360-degree rotating images that let children examine every angle.

Need to know: Reading is minimal, and the interactive features vary from item to item. One favorite is the ability to tweet a message using a World War II Enigma Machine.

Journeys of Invention ©2015 Touchpress. Used with permission.

How to use it: Remember when you used to flip through printed encyclopedia, just browsing pictures? This is the digital equivalent.

Social Play

Some apps are more fun to play alone, and others work well with a friend. The best ones give you a challenge that you can do together. Here are some apps that may foster social relationships.

Curious Words, by Curious Hat (www.curioushat.com); for iPad, iPhone, and iPod Touch; for ages six to eight.

On the plus side: Easy to use and potentially powerful, this creativity experience is like the video-creation app Vine for preschoolers. They are presented with a random word, such as *animal* or *fast*, and are asked to record a one-second video before being prompted by the next word. The entire process is fast and easy, and the app keeps children moving and creating. The short movie is finalized when all the words are recorded and assembled with voiceover and music.

Need to know: Swipe the word up, down, or diagonally to change the voice or camera effect.

How to use it: This would be a great activity for a group of children.

Toca Hair Salon Me, by Toca Boca (http://tocaboca.com), for iPad or iPhone, ages three and up.

On the plus side: This app lets a child's face appear on a customer getting a haircut. Children can become barbers with dozens of tools at their fingertips. They can try out curlers, colored dies, blow-dryers, and so on. The sophisticated face morphing can provide lifelike features, making this a highly social experience.

Need to know: Show children how to line up the eyes and mouth.

Video review: http://youtu.be/7Bg0Lxyjl8o

Toca Hair Salon Me ©2015 Toca Boca. Used with permission.

Storest, by Pixle (www.pixle.pl), for iPad, ages six to eight.

On the plus side: Turn your iPad into a food market scanner, with this innovative shopping simulator. There are two modes of play; one with the camera, the other without. First you visit the store, where you drag and drop items into your shopping cart. Next, you drag and drop the items onto a checkout counter to have them automatically scanned. Children can print out images of products with bar codes and images of shelves that fold to hold their merchandise. They can then fill their baskets, scan the bar codes using the iPad's front camera (with the iPad lying flat), and count up the money when they complete their purchases.

Need to know: You'll need to do some advance setup work printing out the food items and having children cut them out. The prices use the notation style of commas between the ones and decimal places (which is common in many other countries) instead of periods. To accommodate different monetary systems, the prices do not have dollar signs either.

How to use it: This app could be used to set up a physical store in a preschool or child care setting.

FingerPaint Duel, by Cribster (www.foldapps.com), for iPad, for ages six to eight.

On the plus side: This playful drawing game has you sitting face-to-face with another player, with the iPad between you. You each see the same target and

FingerPaint Duel ©2015 Cribster/FoldApps. Used with permission.

race to see who can most accurately color it in. The player who most accurately and quickly replicates the target gets the higher score. The app can store up to fifteen player profiles, each with a picture.

Need to know: This app provides a new type of mediated play on an iPad. The game sets the challenge, acts as an objective scorekeeper, and manages the players' progress.

Note that there are two versions of the app: a lite version and the more expensive EDU version reviewed here.

Kapu Blocks, by Kapu Toys (www.kaputoys.com/en); for iPad, iPhone, and Android; ages five and under.

On the plus side: This playful building activity lets children control a crane that can be used to stack parts of buildings, boats, or hamburgers. The parts must be accurately lined up (an easy process) or they fall into the ocean. A suggested structure is shown as a ghost image, but you don't have to follow the plan. Because the app has two sets of controls, two players can take turns.

Need to know: Younger children could become frustrated by the touch-and-hold claw controls. However, this is an excellent fine motor exercise.

Paint Double, by ambiApps (http://www.ambiapps.com/), for iPad or iPhone, ages five and under.

Paint Double ©2015 Ambi Apps. Used with permission.

On the plus side: Incredibly simple, yet rather random, this painting app draws an imaginary line down the center of the screen, making it easy to make symmetrical doodles. The color changes with each touch, so the child can quickly fill the screen with senseless but pretty doodles. It's just as easy to clear it.

Need to know: On an iPad 3, the retinal display version lagged. The lower-res version on an iPad Mini was better.

Programming

Children don't learn how to code overnight; they need experience playing with commands, sprites, loops, and so on.

Code Studio, by Code.org (www.code.org), for multiple Internet browsers, ages five to fourteen.

On the plus side: This browser-based online learning platform is designed to teach the basics of programming. It is a key part of the code.org initiative, launched to try to get computer programming into every school.

Free content (no registration required) includes six self-guided, online tutorials with video lectures by tech role models such as Bill Gates and Mark Zuckerberg, plus game-based activities designed around popular games such as Angry Birds, Plants vs. Zombies, and Flappy Bird. Features include a Play Lab that lets you send programs to a cell phone via a text message.

The actual coding resembles MIT's Scratch—you drag blocks that represent commands into place to see what they do. Each block snaps into place. The activities are well designed and guide you through each part of the process, step-by-step, until you've reached the hour of code goal.

Need to know: Code Studio works in Flash on most mainstream browsers. A good Internet connection is required.

How to use it: Do this together with the child.

The Foos, by CodeSpark (www.codespark.org); for iPad, iPhone, Android, Amazon Kindle Fire, Mac OSX, and Internet browsers; ages six to eight.

On the plus side: Easy to learn and full of playful characters, this early programming experience mixes an Angry Birds type of leveling system with Scratch-style programming icons. To move your Foo character across the screen to a star, you must drag and drop the correct sequence of commands in the right order. Everything happens in real time, so it's easy to experiment. There's also a handy stick of dynamite—just in case.

Need to know: It's not clear how this free app makes money, or if the .org in the domain means that CodeSpark is a nonprofit. I suspect that future levels will be sold for a fee.

The Foos ©2015 CodeSpark. Used with permission.

Lightbot Jr. 4+ Coding Puzzles, by Lightbot (http://lightbot.com/); for iPad, iPhone, and Android; ages four to eight.

On the plus side: Lightbot is a 3D spatial programming puzzle game that asks children to move a small robot through a stack of blocks using simple forward, turn, and jump commands.

This version, called Lightbot Jr., provides easier puzzles and more help. The forty-two puzzles start with simple forward, backward, right, and left moves, and advance to loops, where a function block can be used to represent a cluster of commands. The looping music can be muted at any time.

Scratch 2.0, by Scratch (http://scratch.mit.edu/), for Windows and Mac OSX, ages seven and up.

On the plus side: This update to the Scratch programming language uses bits of code that snap together like jigsaw puzzles, bringing programming within reach of novices. With this version, you no longer need to download or install anything, and it works best with a traditional Mac or Windows computer, with an Internet connection, browser, and Flash. The language has been enhanced with additional sensors that use your webcam or microphone to detect motion or sound.

Need to know: Because Android tablets can run Flash, it is possible to view existing projects. However, most are designed for using a computer with a mouse and cursor. Scratch 2.0 is a welcome new option, and you certainly can't argue with the free price.

Keeping Up with Changes

Tools for learning and play are constantly changing in our world, and those based on technology are changing even faster. Therefore, it pays to find reliable sources of information on trends and to learn how individual children are using apps and other technological tools.

Some adults take the view that when children are playing with apps or other forms of screen-based media, they're not learning. Children are always learning, but some digital experiences contain more learning possibilities than others. Richer learning experiences contain new challenges that are not too easy and not too hard. They may serve as a catalyst for social interactions that may not have been possible with traditional materials. Screen-sharing experiences such as Skype serve as one example.

If you want to find out what is piquing a child's interest, learn to watch and listen. Any parent who has checked their child's pockets before washing clothes knows how fun it is to find the many interesting items left behind. These treasures each offer a clue about what the child did throughout the day. Similarly, a tablet or a browser contains clues that can help you retrace the child's steps.

You can see which websites or topics interest a child by checking the browser history, which will show recent sites visited. Be alert if there is no history. This may mean that the child has figured out how to use the private mode, which isn't tracked, or how to clear the browser's cache, erasing his steps.

On an Android tablet, you can see which apps a child has been using by tapping the recent apps button. On an iPad, you can double-tap the home button to see open apps. This option will show iPad apps running in the background because they haven't been shut down completely.

Once you know which apps are capturing children's attention, you can build on those interests, keep the existing apps updated, and add more, as appropriate.

Managing Your App Library

Once upon a time, you went to a store and purchased a book, tape, disk, or game cartridge. It was yours to keep forever, as long as the device for playing it kept working.

Today with services such as Amazon.com, Google Play, and iTunes, we do not need CDs, cartridges, and hard disks anymore. But you must have access to the Internet. You purchase the right to download the content and any updates to it, forever. So what if the publisher goes out of business? You're out of business, too. But remember that when you pay for a code, you own it for life. That $0.99 copy of Doodle Jump that you invested in five years ago is still yours, for any future device you might have. The app stores usually have limits on the number of devices that can play an app at one time. Check your account information to see which devices you have listed.

Buying New Apps

As you consider the price of a particular app, keep in mind that free apps can have hidden costs. The limited content can inspire frustration in children and lead them to feel tricked. This is a waste of something very precious—a child's energy. Children quickly learn which apps are worth their time. By carefully screening free apps that offer only a sample of content and treating them with skepticism, you can help keep children from becoming distracted and disappointed.

As soon as the child starts shopping for apps, consider setting up an individual iTunes or Google Play account. Help the child pick out a screen name and password that is easy to remember but is secure. This is a good time to talk with children about security issues and issues related to sharing information. Make sure you record their screen names and passwords. Next, purchase a gift card for the app store, and credit the child's account. This protects you from the liability of having a credit card. It also helps children better understand how to manage resources. Make sure to check the child's apps frequently, helping to organize the icons. Note that with iTunes, it's possible to log in with your account and download apps you've already purchased. The child's apps won't disappear, as long as you're within your limit on the number of devices for the app.

Keeping Your Apps Updated

You can tell when a loaf of bread gets stale with a squeeze. For apps, you'll need to find the updates menu. On an iPad or iPhone, you will know that your app has an update available if you see a little red bubble with a number on the app icon. That means a new version is available. To update your app, go to your app store icon and select the update option. Tap each icon to start the download or update all. You can also set up your tablet to automatically update when it is connected to wi-fi. On Android devices, you can get alerts about app updates on the notifications screen.

Deleting an App

If you want to delete an app because you are running low on space or just don't like it, you can do that, too. On an iPad, you can go to the home screen and touch the app icon, holding your finger on it until it starts to wiggle. Touch the little X in the corner of the icon to delete it, and confirm the deletion. On an Android, you will need to go to the settings feature, which usually looks like a cog wheel. Find the apps section, and tap the app you want to delete. You should see an uninstall option, and you can tap that button and confirm. Help children develop these app-management skills, so they can manage their own devices, independently.

More Tips and Tricks

As a parent, you will likely want to be prepared to minimize the negative possibilities that accompany children's use of tablets and smartphones and to capitalize on the potential benefits.

Setting Guidelines

When you're spending time with family or you are out in a restaurant, tablets and cell phones may be an unwelcome distraction. You can lead by example. Consider instituting rules about leaving devices in the car. Remember that asking a child not to use a tablet or phone is easier said than done. You can also consider setting a timer that limits the time with the device. It's best to focus on the child's behavior and give the child choices. Overall, you will need to set firm guidelines and stick to them.

Movie Downloads

If you know you're going to be traveling where you will not have wi-fi access and you want to have some favorite videos to play, you will need to plan ahead. You can purchase movies and songs as you purchase apps and then download them. Keep in mind, however, that movies can be much bigger than apps; the high-definition version of *Toy Story 3* is about 4.32 GB. Movies also can be expensive. But you can keep the movie in your account and download it in the future on any device. If you're headed for a long trip, don't leave your downloading to the last minute.

Google Cardboard Virtual-Reality Viewers

Virtual-reality (or VR) goggles (such as the Samsung Galaxy Gear, Oculus, or Sony VR) are amazing, but they can cost hundreds of dollars and might require specific software. They also can require a specific computer or game console. Google Cardboard, on the other hand, is an option that costs less than $20 and provides a similar experience by leveraging the power of your mobile phone. A Google Cardboard certified viewer (https://www.google.com/get/cardboard/get-cardboard/) can be assembled out of cardboard. These viewers combine lenses with cardboard or other materials, and they work with Apple or Android smartphones.

Concerns about Young Children and Technology

Discussions about screens and children bring out strong and varied emotions among parents, teachers, librarians, and pediatricians, in part because the devices are so relatively new. Consider that in all of human history, no other generation has seen so much technology-driven change, and adjusting to it is not optional.

Myths and Guidance

BUCKLEITNER RECOMMENDS

Misconceptions about children and technology use continue to pop up. Here are some common thoughts and concerns, with my advice:

- **Glowing screens can turn children into asocial nerds.** It depends entirely on which video game or app is making the screen glow. Experiences such as Nintendo's Mario Party or Toca Hair Salon Me present unique social opportunities.

- **Using computers will make children smarter.** Clearly, quality apps can be powerful learning tools, and they can even provide practice with some preacademic skills. But no teacher or app can teach children concepts that they are not developmentally ready for. For instance, a preschooler may be frustrated with an app that focuses on reading and short words. She might be ready for an app that provides light exposure to prereading skills with letter recognition, shape matching, and lots of touch-and-hear-style interaction. Remember that children learn best when exposed to many different types of experiences. Video games, computers, mobile phones, browsers, and tablets loaded with apps should be considered a supplement to more concrete learning activities such as completing puzzles, building with blocks and Lego bricks, reading books, creating art projects, and playing outside on the playground.

- **Tablets and technology will make printed books obsolete.** These are very different types of experiences. Because a story presented on a screen can be interactive, the mind is working in a different way than with a printed book. Reading a printed book is a linear process, and the work takes place in your mind. A book leaves more room for the imagination but does not in itself provide types of play that might extend the story in unique ways. You will find that e-books can work on a continuum from interactive to noninteractive. In some cases, you can find an app that works with the printed page to further extend the author's telling of the story, as Moonbot Studios' IMAG•N•O•TRON app does with *The Fantastic Flying Books of Mr. Morris Lessmore* by William Joyce.

- **Sitting close to screens will damage a child's eyes.** Continual reading on digital screens requires precautions just as print reading does, according to the

American Optometric Association (AOA). The lighting, glare, viewing distance, seating posture, and uncorrected vision problems can affect symptoms of eye strain, an AOA online article notes, but the symptoms tend to be temporary. Some research has shown that people tend to stare more and blink less on digital screens, which can contribute to dry eyes. Doctors, therefore, recommend frequent breaks to look away from the screen as well as using proper lighting and positioning while reading. James Salz, a University of Southern California eye doctor and spokesperson for the American Academy of Ophthalmology, noted in a 2014 *Washington Post* article by Jill Adams that "there's no evidence that there's any long-term damage from reading on a screen."

How Much Screen Time Is Too Much?

Being a caregiver or parent of a young child can be exhausting. When you mix in some unknowns such as children's seemingly unnatural attraction to glowing screens, the challenges can be bewildering. Many adults wonder: what is the right mix of apps and grass stains?

Although the answer is subjective, a 2012 joint position statement from the National Association for the Education of Young Children (NAEYC) and the Fred Rogers Center for Early Learning and Children's Media discusses the use

of technology and interactive media in early childhood programs. The document addresses many of the concerns and controversies involved with raising a young child in the digital age. Note that I was one of the many advisors to the document, so I know it well. The key guidelines focus on three words: access, balance, and support—or ABS, just like your car's brake system.

A is for access. Children won't gain technology competence if they can't touch the technology. Preschools and child care environments can provide access to children who do not have the technology at home. By playing or fiddling around with digital cameras, downloading apps, using laptops, and playing video game systems, they will figure out how to wiggle a connection to make something work, find a wi-fi signal to avoid roaming charges, or get a song from a CD to a file. By the time they reach middle school, they will be bilingual, fluent in both Windows and Mac, and they can pick up a Chromebook, a Kindle, or an iPad with no hesitation.

B is for balance. Just as a healthy diet consists of a variety of foods, a child needs the right mix of concrete and abstract, real and pretend. Screens tend to be abstract and symbolic, so screen time should be balanced with real and concrete activities.

This can be easier said than done when a child is immersed in a digital game or app. There's an art to knowing when to set a limit or when to play along. You might take your child camping in a state park in the summer, but rather than leave your iPad behind, you could use the Star Walk app to find stars or use the camera to capture the sunset. The screen can make a pretty good nightlight too, but no app can replace the experience of singing songs with the family around a campfire.

S is for support. Left on their own, young children won't be able to get access to technology and achieve balance. They need an expert like you and other adults in their life who can tune into their abilities and interests. Support can come in the form of friends, siblings, parents, grandparents, librarians, and teachers, who might serve as fearless technology role models, bedtime story readers, app curators, and helpers for reaching those hard game levels.

If you try your best to create the ABS formula while children are young, someday they might be able to record and edit a video for a class project, best their parent's score in Super Mario Bros., program a sprite in Scratch, find and download a calculus app, use online banking, post prom pictures on social media, and—more important—have the wisdom to know when not to post something.

Next time you hear a car dealer talking about an antilock braking system, remember the other meaning of ABS. Both can keep you out of the ditch and on your way to your destination.

Go with the Flow: Strategies for Limiting Screen Time

Before shutting down the tablet in frustration when a child appears to be a digital addict, take time to understand why the child is glued to the screen. Try to observe the rhythm of the play so you understand the task. You might even consider playing along or offering your help. Consider these tips for setting limits:

- Give advance notice that the time is almost up, and follow through. You might say, "In five minutes we shut down the tablet." If possible, use an egg timer so the child can visualize the time remaining. Be aware that if you give a warning but don't stick to it, the credibility of your words will fade.

- Put the time limit into the context of the activity children are immersed in. Tell them they have time for two more puzzles, one more level, or one last picture.

- Ask them to push the button to stop the action instead of doing it yourself. Giving children control over making the experience end can help them more peacefully accept the consequences. This button might be the power button on a remote, the pause option on a video game, or the home button on an iPad. This gives children the active role in ending the activity and somehow helps them internalize the process. When the screen image

disappears, it is almost magical how you get the child to interact with you again.

• As a parent, try to involve yourself in your child's intense interest and worry less about it. Children naturally go through periods when they are intensely interested in an app, game, or topic. Mark Zuckerberg and Bill Gates also might have appeared to be computer addicts at one point.

Protecting Children from Violence on Screens

Some apps, video games, or news programs might give children nightmares. Fortunately, Fred Rogers (known as Mr. Rogers on TV) gave a great deal of thought to this issue, especially just after the September 11, 2001, terrorist attacks in the United States. (Fred Rogers died in 2003.) Although TVs were smaller then, his advice still rings true.

On his company's website (www.fredrogers.org) on a page called Tragic Events, Rogers advised parents to turn off the TV when children are around, especially when there's a breaking news story, and to honestly acknowledge that as adults, we are struggling with our own feelings. During tragic events, he said, children need time with the adults in their lives, away from frightening images on the news.

Rogers reminded us that play is one of the important ways young children have of dealing with their concerns. "When children are scared and anxious, they might become more dependent, clingy, and afraid to go to bed at night," he said. "Whining, aggressive behavior, or toilet 'accidents' may be their way of asking for more comfort from the important adults in their lives."

Children notice when the adults in their lives are worried. So you might admit feeling bad about those images, too, and letting children know that you have chosen not to watch the videos or newscasts.

Limiting Access to YouTube Videos

Not only are you a role model for the children in your life, but oftentimes, you are also their protector. In this role, it makes sense to set restrictions on the types of videos they can see.

To change the YouTube settings, start the YouTube app, go to your profile, and find the settings gear. Check the filtering, and set it to moderate or strict.

You can also set up restrictions for blocking a browser or YouTube access altogether behind a four-digit PIN code. Search online to find the specific directions for your tablet.

After changing the settings, you can check them by starting the YouTube app and typing in the name of a few R-rated video games, such as Medal of Honor or

Halo, or an inappropriate search term that older children might use. Then you can see what turns up in the search results.

Fun Activities to Try with Google

- Type the word *tilt* in the Google search line. This search is one of many playful hidden treasures (programmers call them *Easter eggs*) hidden inside Google. It makes your screen tilt to one side. Another fun trick is to type *do a barrel roll* and watch the screen flip around.

- Search your own first and last name, first in quotes and then without quotes, to illustrate the power of searching for an exact string.

- Use Image mode (http://images.google.com/), and find your own backyard.

- Play with Google Earth (http://www.google.com/earth) and Google Moon (http://www.google.com/moon).

- Create a Gmail account for your child (mail.google.com). Be sure to pick a screen name that is easy to remember but secure.

- Explore the Google Doodles (http://www.google.com/doodles/), which offer more than 2,000 playful or history-inspired renditions of the Google logo.

- Search with your voice. Click on the microphone icon in the search window and say "flip a coin."

- Translate something from one language to another using Google Translate (www.translate.google.com).

Fun Questions for Siri, Alexa, or Cortana

Hold down the Home button on a newer iPad or iPhone for a few seconds, and you might start Siri, Apple's famous talking assistant. It turns out that talking to a machine is an excellent way for a child to practice spoken language, as well as to interact with a computer using voice.

The following questions should elicit interesting responses from Siri:

- "Will I need my raincoat tomorrow?" Siri will tell you the weather forecast for wherever you are.

- "Where am I?" Siri can tell you the location.

- "What's 2 + 2?" Siri is very good at math.

- "Will you marry me?" Siri comes back with a random, snappy answer.

- "Why did the chicken cross the road?" Siri has an answer.

- "How much wood would a woodchuck chuck if a woodchuck could chuck wood?" If you can say it, Siri has the answer.

- "What is the meaning of life?" Siri has the answer.

- "I love you." Siri reminds you that he or she is a machine.

Other things to say to Siri include: "Call me (say your name)," to rename your phone or iPad. "Do not disturb," to silence any sounds. "What's the capital of North Dakota?"— Siri is really good at geography questions. "Set a timer for 10 minutes"—Siri will start a countdown that you can use to remind a child when it's time to turn off the screen. Note that these same questions work well with other voice-driven assistants, such as Microsoft's Cortana or Amazon's Alexa.

Conclusion

For generations, parents have learned to watch for well-established developmental milestones, such as learning to walk, talk, and ride a bicycle. That is certain. Much more uncertain is the degree to which digital technology can influence a developing child in either positive or negative ways; both outcomes are open to interpretation.

Today we enjoy technologies that were the dreams of yesterday's generation, offering countless possibilities to improve the quality of childhood. The job for parents and educators is to match quality technology-based experiences to each child.

I have shared many ideas with you in this book, but I would like to end where we started. At the very dawn of educational technology, when the potential of microprocessors offered endless blue-sky ideas about learning, educators and philosophers were intrigued. One of these philosophers was Patrick Suppes, a Stanford professor, who in 1966 predicted, "In a few more years, millions of school children will have access to what Philip of Macedon's son Alexander enjoyed as a royal prerogative: the personal services of a tutor as well informed and as responsive as Aristotle."

Today, the power Suppes predicted is here. We can hand children an affordable, durable device with a screen that can display the finest art, speakers that can play the greatest symphonies, day-long batteries, and a search engine that can answer many questions. But choosing the apps and unlocking this potential is easier said than done. I hope that this book will help.

REFERENCES AND RESOURCES

Adams, Jill U. 2014. "How Bad for Your Eyes Are Computer Screens?"
    The Washington Post, January 20. https://www.washingtonpost.com
    /national/health-science/how-bad-for-your-eyes-are-computer
    -screens/2014/01/17/985b90cc-7c98-11e3-93c1-0e888170b723_story.html

AOA. 2015. *Computer Vision Syndrome,* accessed November 6, 2015.
    http://www.aoa.org/patients-and-public/caring-for-your-vision
    /protecting-your-vision/computer-vision-syndrome?sso=y

Buckleitner, Warren. 2014. "Protecting Children from Extreme Screen Violence."
    Fred Rogers Center. http://www.fredrogerscenter.org/blog/protecting
    -children-from-extreme-screen-violence

Markoff, John. 2014. "Patrick Suppes, Pioneer in Computerized Learning, Dies at
    92." *New York Times*, December 3. http://www.nytimes.com/2014/12/03/us
    /patrick-suppes-pioneer-in-computerized-learning-dies-at-92.html

NAEYC and the Fred Rogers Center for Early Learning and Children's Media
    at Saint Vincent College. 2012. *Technology and Interactive Media as
    Tools in Early Childhood Programs Serving Children from Birth through
    Age 8*. Position statement. http://www.naeyc.org/content
    /technology-and-young-children

Rogers, Fred. 2015. "Tragic Events." *The Fred Rogers Co.*, accessed September 15,
    2015. http://www.fredrogers.org/parents/special-challenges
    /tragic-events.php

INDEX

J